A VAGABOND IN THE CAUCASUS

Stephen Graham's *A Vagabond in the Caucasus* is a supremely unique take on travel through Russia and the Caucasus. Graham takes to the road in a modest fashion, with a bag and his camera at his side. As he arrives in Moscow not long after the Russian Revolution in 1917 he is not entirely welcomed with open arms. Instead, Graham is greeted by a group of soldiers as he walks down the street and is arrested on the spot. He recounts this experience, as well as every moment of his time spent 'vagabonding' across the Caucasus with glorious detail.

His photographs to accompany the text capture the fleeting moments of this politically heated time in Russia with candid accuracy. In one image, ragged women from a beer house slum pose on their front steps: Some with sneering disregard for the camera, others proud to be the subject of Graham's composition. The shot is nearly ruined by the blurred figure of what looks to be a Russian soldier passing on his beat. It is moments like these, where various aspects of culture in the Caucasus cross paths, that are so gracefully captured by Graham, between his great stories and his dedicated photography. This momentous work is not to be overlooked by anyone interested in travel or history, or anyone with a taste for an unconventional account of the land of the Caucasus.

TOMB OF A CAUCASIAN CHIEF, SHOWING WHAT HE DIED POSSESSED OF INCLUDING THE ACTUAL NUMBER OF HIS CARTRIDGES

A VAGABOND IN THE CAUCASUS

SOME NOTES OF HIS EXPERIENCES AMONG THE RUSSIANS

STEPHEN GRAHAM

LONDON AND NEW YORK

First published 2005 by
Kegan Paul limited

Published 2013 by Routledge
2 Park Square, Milton Park, Abingdon, Oxfordshire OX14 4RN
711 Third Avenue, New York, NY 10017, USA

First issued in paperback 2016

Routledge is an imprint of the Taylor & Francis Group, an informa business

ISBN 13: 978-1-138-98664-0 (pbk)
ISBN 13: 978-0-7103-1145-0 (hbk)

British Library Cataloguing in Publication Data

Library of Congress Cataloging-in-Publication Data
Applied for.

CONTENTS

ILLUSTRATIONS

MAPS

A VAGABOND IN THE CAUCASUS

A

NOTE

Portions of Chapters VI., VII., IX., XI., XXVIII. appeared originally in articles contributed to *Country Life*, and Chapter XXII. and parts of II., X., XXXIII. in articles contributed to the *Pall Mall Gazette*, to the Editors of which journals the author desires to make all due acknowledgment.

A VAGABOND IN THE CAUCASUS

PROLOGUE

HOW I CAME TO BE A TRAMP

I BROUGHT myself up on Carlyle and found him the dearest, gentlest, bravest, noblest man. The Life by Froude was dearer to me than the Gospel of St Matthew, or Hamlet, or Macbeth, and that is saying much if the reader only knew me. Carlyle was so near that I saw him in dreams and spoke with him in words that were true, unquestionably. In the vision world of my dream he behaved exactly as he would have done in real life, I am sure of it. He was flesh and blood to me. Yet he died and was buried before I was born. How strange! This man who died three years before I was born was a friend closer to me than a lover, one to whom I longed to say caressing words, one whom I longed to embrace and fondle—to kiss even.

He made me work, the dear, irascible, eloquent old

sage. I worked at his bidding and set myself impossible tasks—impossible! I became a puritan, serious, intolerant and heroic; and in moments of rapture, conscious of the silence of the stars and the graves, I would sing to the night the marching song:

> "Here eyes do regard you
> In Eternity's stillness,
> Here is all fulness,
> Ye brave, to reward you,
> Work and despair not."

Carlyle was a true friend to me, he was not content that he only should be my friend, I had to become the friend of his friends. Now, I am one of the Great Society of his friends. I belong to the fellowship of those that have seen The City. The Great Society has among its members many children and many jolly tramps. Has the reader ever been introduced personally to the Great Ones long since dead? I think these literary men the great Friends of Mankind. They allow themselves to be known and cherished—different from military heroes or scientists or explorers. One would as soon love a waxwork as Napoleon. Yet even the despised and rejected of the literary world are warm and smiling friends to their readers. I, for my part, adored Ruskin and Browning as a young girl in love with a new history mistress. I obeyed Ruskin, bought his works in purple calf and looked up the long words in the dictionary. Then Rabbi Ben Ezra entered into me so that I spoke with tongues. I learned the poem by heart and recited it to sunsets. I ask myself now how I reconciled " Work and despair not " with

> " Not on the vulgar mass,
> Called work must sentence pass."

But of course both sentences are true; one is for one nature, the other for another; I think I must have really belonged to the second category, for have I not become a tramp!

I never felt so humanly close to Ruskin as to Carlyle. He had a way of stating *the truth.* He liked to perch on his truths and crow. No, I revered him, but decidedly didn't like him. Browning made friends with me. Then came Ibsen; and both Browning and Ibsen confirmed me in the heroism of achieving impossible tasks. Has the reader seen the " Master Builder," the man who did the impossible twice? " It's—fearfully thrilling." In these days I spouted: " Life is like the compound eye of the fly. It is full of lives. Momentarily we died, momentarily are born again. The old self dies, the new is born; the old life gives way to the new. The selfish man wishes to remain as he is; in his life are fewer lives, fewer changes. But the hero wishes to fulfil every promise written in his being. He dies gladly in each moment to arise the next moment more glorious, nearer to perfection. Oh, my friend, pay for the new life with all the old. The life that thou hast, was given thee for paying away so that thou mightest obtain something better."

In myself I believed these words. I worked and read. I worked and threw myself at the impossible. What Swinburne wrote is true:

> " A joy to the heart of a man
> Is a goal that he may not reach."

I wrote lectures in which my style was so infected by the rhetoric of the sage that listeners grumbled that they could not tell when I was quoting and when I was using my own language. That was their defect; they should have known Carlyle better! One lecture I specially remember. It was given to some Essex folk. It related to Hero-worship. All the artillery of Carlyle was in play. It was a subject supremely Carlylean. Work, I praised, and heroic valour. But my message was: " In each of you there is a Hero, let him out; in each man there is a Hero, see one there," which is not what Carlyle meant when he said: " Recognise the Hero when you see him and obey." This was, perhaps, a first divergency. Carlyle was looking for a means to govern a nation wisely. I was moving towards my tramp destiny.

That was in the year of the Russian Revolution and I had been learning Russian very sedulously for some time. A literary ambition had possession of me. I had said to myself—one must specialise to get on in the world of literature. Carlyle specialised German. German things did not interest me. I had long since learned to enjoy Turgeniev and Gorky and Gogol in English translations, and Russia had become to me the most interesting country in Europe. I determined to specialise on Russia.

Yes, and when, according to the newspapers, the bombs were flying thick and fast, I took a return ticket for Moscow and went out. For luggage I took a camera and a small hand-bag. The tramp has the soberest conscience about luggage. He feels he can always *do without*. But, of course, I wasn't a tramp then. I may remark in passing that I lost none of that luggage and had no trouble whatever with it. Few travellers manage their first trip to Russia without vexatious misadventures. On one occasion, however, when I was taking a snap-shot of a prison, a soldier rushed up to me in terror and rage. He thought my Kodak was a bomb.

What an excitement this journey was! I had never even been abroad before. Now I went through Holland and across the whole of Germany and into Poland. Two days after I had left England I was in Russia. I arrived at Warsaw on the day the Governor was shot. I saw at once there were more soldiers than people in the streets. I took a droschky to a hotel, put down my things and strolled out to see the city. I was arrested at once. Fifty yards down Marzalkovsky, the Piccadilly of Warsaw, a soldier stopped me, searched me and handed me over to an officer and six armed guards. I was put in the middle and marched off; on each side of me a soldier held a drawn sword and was ready to slash at me if I should attempt to bolt. I am sure the angels wept. Internally I collapsed with laughter and at the same time I felt very rich. I was having an experience.

I was released and was arrested again, and a Circassian guard punched me in the stomach very hard, " for luck," I think he said. They gave an account of my arrest in the *Russ* and said I had been nearly beaten to death, but they didn't know who I was. Somehow it came to England as the arrest and flogging of Mr Foster Fraser, the well-known correspondent. Poor Mr Fraser, it must have been awkward explaining to his friends that it was not really he who was flogged.

I was not a correspondent, but I wrote of my adventures, and it was very pleasant to see my words printed in London newspapers. It was very amusing to see myself styled " Our own Special Correspondent," when, in truth, I was only a free lance and had not even seen the face of a London editor. Journalism is a cheap trade! At Warsaw I met correspondents of many papers and had surprising glimpses behind the scenes. There was a little American Jew there who knew almost every language in Europe, who had an eye for every nationality, and who knew the private history of all the women of the city. At one time he had been hotel tout,

HARBOUR, NIZHNI NOVGOROD

OUTSIDE A SLUM BEERHOUSE, MOSCOW

interpreter, guide, but now was correspondent, reporter, supplier of information. He was always hanging about the chief hotel and watching for journalists hard up for copy. There were crowds of English newspaper men who could not speak intelligibly in French, far less in Russian. To such the American was a god-send. And Lord, what stories they wrote home to England!

I left Warsaw for Moscow and Nizhni. When I left the American was a lonely bachelor. When I returned his wife had found him. She told me her story. She lost her man in New York and had chased him through the States, and through Europe. He was always giving her the slip. I think my trembling puritanism rose to the defence of my innocent soul. Life is of all colours, but there are some terrible reds and scarlets one doesn't see in England. Warsaw to me was a wicked city. The wonderful beauty of Polish girls I had then no eyes for.

I returned to England and was a local lion.

The trip brought me pleasant glory, but it had given me powerful hopes and longings. I had been in the Kremlin and in the churches. I had been a vagabond at the Fair of Nizhni Novgorod. I had seen the peasants and their faces and eyes and lives. I learned many things from these peasant faces. I said to myself at Moscow: "These people are like what English people were when Edward the Third was king." Of a face passing I would say to myself: "There are three or four hundred years behind that nose and mouth and eyes and chin." The irresistible question came: "Are these peasants not better off than the English clerk or labourer?" As a question I left it.

England again! I returned, for I had an appointment there, comfortable though not literary. Life had good things in store for me there—more reading, new acquaintances, a new Friend even. I took up Russian more seriously and commenced a translation of a novel of Dostoievsky. I was learning to know others of that Great Society, and one day the Fates brought me to Zarathustra. I was an unruly candidate for a place in the society of the "free, very free spirits," but a true candidate.

Puritanism and intolerance were now to be attacked. A thawing wind began to blow upon the winter of my discontent. "Convictions are prisons," I read. And surely I was imprisoned behind many prison walls. I was in the centre of a labyrinth of convictions and principles. I believed in work and, at the same time, I believed in myself. Neitzsche reinforced the belief in myself. I was doing work that was not congenial. I was in work that imprisoned me and that prevented development. I was longing for the new. Still in my heart lived the sentences: "Do the impossible, pay for the New with all the Old."

I wanted new life, broader horizons, deeper depths, higher heights. I knew these might be purchased by giving up my appointment in London and throwing myself into Russia. Yes, to go to Russia and live there, that was my next step. I came to that conclusion one Sunday in June. In one little moment I made that big decision. The tiniest seed was sown in Time. The Fates stood by, the seed lived. To-day that seed is bearing the finest blossoms. May each chapter here be a garland of its flowers exhaling their life perfume.

I shaped my plans to the end.

> "'A Yea, a Nay
> A straight line
> A Goal'—saith Zarathustra."

My Yea was Russia; my Nay, England; the straight line, the nearest way, my Goal, the new life to be paid for with all the old.

In London I had made a Russian acquaintance, the son of a deacon of the Orthodox Church, and just before my departure I received an invitation to spend Christmas at Lisitchansk, a village some way north of the Sea of Azov, some miles south of Kharkov. Russia had seemed dark, enigmatical, terrible, but here at the last minute arms stretched out of the darkness, welcoming me, alluring me.

On what was Old Year's Night in England, though in Russia only the eighteenth of December, I was at Dover. The lights of the harbour shone on the placid water. The stars looked down upon my starting, the same stars that were at that moment looking down upon my destination also, my stars, the stars that through all my wanderings have shone down. One Friend bade me farewell. At Dover, on the ship in the harbour in the night, we embraced and parted. England herself grasped my hand and bade me farewell. For a moment, in the stillness, the sea ceased to exist and space was gone—Two hands were clasped between the lands.

My life as a wanderer began. I might say my life as a tramp began, for I never worked again. I became, as the philosopher says, " full of malice against the seductions of dependency that lie concealed in houses, money or positions." Whereas I had sold myself to work, I had now bought myself back, I had exchanged dependence upon man for dependence upon God, and had given up my respectable West - End home in " Berkeley Square," so that I might take up my abode in the West End of this Universe.

Perhaps not then, but now I ask: " Could anything be more amusing than the modern cry of the Right to Work? The English are an industrious, restless nation. And the prophets are very censorious of our respectable, though not respected, class. " It is not enough to be industrious," says Thoreau ; " so are the ants. The question is, What are you industrious about ? " No one questions the use of industry of one kind or another. Dear Carlyle, my guide, philosopher and friend, I wonder if he, in other realms, has learned the value of idleness. Perhaps now, after a life-time of Nirvana in some Eden planet, he has smoothed out his ruffled soul. Oh, friends, there are depths of calm and happiness to be found even here, and not autumn stillness but spring calm, the joyful peace of the dove brooding on the waters. I have learned to smooth and compose a rough, tumbled mind until it was like a broad, unsullied mirror reflecting the beauty of the world.

Two thousand miles from London there are new silences, pregnant stillness, on the steppes, in the country places, on the skirts of the old forests. No word of the hubbub of democracy need come through; not a hoarding poster flaunts the eye; no burning question of the hour torments the mind. A man is master of himself and may see or hear or consider just what he chooses. That is, if the man be like me.

"You look up at the sky, as you lie under a bush, and it keeps descending, descending to you, as though it wanted to embrace you. . . . Your soul is warm and quietly joyful, you desire nothing, you envy no one."

" . . . And so it seems as though on all the earth there were only you and God. . . ."

"All around is silence: only the birds are singing, and this silence is so marvellous that it seems as though the birds were singing in your own breast." So wrote Gorky, the tramp. I almost wish he would write the story of his vagabondage instead of being so serious over his revolutionary propaganda.

I have shown how I came to be a wanderer. I will now add to this prologue a word of dedication. The prose of this book is the story of my travels; the poetry, when the reader may discern it, is the story of my heart.

CHAPTER I

ROBBED IN THE TRAIN

GERMANY is a safe country. One is not permitted to lose oneself there. I, for my part, knew not a word of German beyond *nicht hinauslehnen*, which means: don't put your head out at the window; but I had no misadventures there. The trains leave punctually, the carriages are all clean, the porters know their duty. One contrast has particularly impressed me. In Russia, in second or even in first-class carriages, washing accommodation is very poor. Often there is no water, and there is seldom a stopper to the hand-basin. There is a murky mirror but no towel, indeed, no further convenience of any kind. In Germany, on the contrary, even third-class accommodation is superb. There is a fresh tablet of soap and a clean towel for each traveller; there is even a comb and brush, if one cares to use them after others. But in Russia third-class accommodation is unspeakably filthy, and I think that if one mentioned the idea of soap gratis to a Russian official he would frown as if overhearing revolutionary propaganda. Surely the Germans have the cleanest faces among all nations, and their free wash seems to say: " For God's sake, don't let a little piece of official soap stand between you and cleanliness."

But though Russian accommodation is inferior in this respect, it has one great excellence: the trains run smoothly over the lines. One can make the whole trans-Siberian journey from Warsaw to Shanghai and be as fit at the end as when one started. The movement of the train is so pleasantly soothing that one slips easily into slumber. Indeed, if one wakes in the night and finds the train stopping in a station, one waits and longs for the train to move again; minutes seem eternities. Then one is entitled by one's ticket to the whole length of a seat. No one objects if one undresses, and at least one can always remove collar, boots and overcoat. But German trains are noisy; they jerk and rattle and tear through the night. They compare with Russian trains as a motor omnibus might with a child's cradle. One would stand more chance of sleeping in the Inner Circle.

I arrived at Alexandrovo, the frontier town, at ten o'clock at night, and took train on for Warsaw at 1 a.m. My luggage was registered through to Kharkov. The customs officer informed me that it had been forwarded and would be examined there. This was on the third day of my journey, and I had had two nights without sleep. It was with a great deal of gladness that I settled myself down in my Russian *coupé* and hoped to sleep a few hours. The third bell, the last bell, sounded, and the train moved slowly out of the station and ground itself away over the heavy, snow-covered track. The guards came and punched my ticket; then I lay back and fell fast asleep. The white train moved over the white fields, and the light wind blew the thick snow against the window panes, or wreathed it in the gangways between the corridors. The train moved very slowly, and every quarter of an hour or so stopped. The movement was very weak and gentle, like the pulsation of an old man's heart. When it ceased, it seemed to have paused through utter exhaustion. I was suddenly awakened by a touch on the shoulder. I opened my eyes and saw a man bending over me. I could have sworn he had been picking my pockets. He smiled unamiably and asked a question in German. Getting no answer he tried Polish; I replied in Russian. He wanted to know where I was going to, and whether I was a German.

This man afterwards robbed me. Next time I woke up my heavy overcoat was gone. I had hung it on a peg beside me, and when I looked for it it had disappeared. And the smiling Pole who had been sitting opposite had also disappeared. New people were in the compartment. In fact, the moment I woke there were two men standing beside me and kissing one another frantically. The train had stopped at a station. I was dazed. I thought I was, perhaps, at Warsaw already. I was assured Warsaw was a long way off, and then I discovered the loss of my coat.

The chief guard assured me the coat would be recovered. If I would give him a rouble he would have the train searched. He took down notes of what I said and pocketed the money, but the thief got clear away. The flickering candle that illuminated the carriage was burning out. It was so dark that one could not be sure whether anything were lost or not. My astonishment was great when I looked under the seat and saw a man lying there—a man with a smell. The guard came in at that moment and we hauled the stowaway out. I thought it was the thief for certain. He was brought out and searched. He was a tatterdemalion, out at knees and out at elbows, thick with grease and dirt. His feet were wrapped up with sacking, tied round with rope, and the rest of his attire was uncured sheepskin. He hadn't any ticket and was going to Warsaw. He offered the guard twopence as a bribe, but the latter frowned terribly and asked whether I would care to have him arrested. He whispered to me aside that he felt quite sure we had caught the thief or an accomplice. If I would give him two roubles he would make a declaration at the next station. I should get my coat in a week at least. But I dissented, for I felt quite sure such a disreputable-looking character as the moujik we had hauled out was incapable of stealing a handsome overcoat. So the guard accepted twopence from the man in lieu of a ticket, and was fain to disappear.

Russian trains are well heated. It is only when one steps out at a station that one realises how cold it is. I soon began to realise what the loss of my coat meant. At Kharkov there were forty degrees of frost. The further into Russia the colder it became. My only protection was a light summer overcoat and a plaid rug. My gloves, together with a voluminous silk muffler, had been left in the pockets of the coat that was stolen. When I went out at Kharkov the cold struck in on all sides, and my moustache and eyebrows froze to solid ice at once.

Calamity followed close upon calamity. My registered luggage was nowhere to be found. The customs officer was of opinion that it had been delayed on the line. If I would leave ten roubles with him he would look after it and forward it some time after Christmas.

The cup of misery seemed filled to the brim. For I was deprived of all my clothes but the rough travelling things I stood up in. I pictured to myself what a strange, shabby Christmas guest I should appear.

It was the 23rd of December, according to the old calendar; the morrow would be Christmas Eve, and all shops would be shut. I went out into the town and made good some of my deficiencies.

I had still a hundred-mile journey to make before I

reached Lisitchansk. The train left at 9 p.m. I telegraphed to my friend, asking to be met, and then went off to buy a ticket. The booking-office clerk would not issue tickets until he could be sure that the train would be run. The last express from Sevastopol had arrived ten hours late.

I waited until midnight, and then at last a notice was put out intimating that the train would start. So I purchased my ticket and took my seat, and at two in the morning we moved slowly out. My impression of that train is that everyone, including passengers, guards and driver, was drunk. It was crowded with people going home for Christmas. It was so crowded that there seemed to be no intention on the part of anyone to sleep, and I could not get a seat to myself. At length, however, a very friendly, though tipsy, Little Russian made an arrangement with the occupants of a ladies' compartment, and I got an upper shelf there to lie upon.

When I awakened it was broad day and the train had stopped finally. A lady on a shelf opposite was reading a novel. No one else seemed to be in the carriage. I learned from her that we were snowed up. All the men employed to keep the line clear were dead drunk. No further progress would be made until after dinner. There was a forest on the right-hand side, full of wolves, the girl said. I went along to the men's compartment and found that everyone had adjourned to a farm-house near by to get dinner. Evidently thieves were not feared in that part of the country. I followed the others to the house and had a good hot dish of cabbage soup. It was a one-room cottage, and was packed with people. The clamour was deafening. I think the family must have had an unusually large supply of vodka, for the number of Christmas healths drunk was at least treble the number of guests.

At about three o'clock the engine-driver, who was so drunk that he could not stand up, was lifted into the engine and he set the train going. Scarcely anyone was in the train, neither people nor guards, and there was a rush to get on. But only about six were successful; the rest were all left behind. We, at the farm-house, had no chance whatever. Somebody said, "The train is starting," and there was a stampede. Every vodka glass was drained, the singing stopped, and the shouting and the step-dancing, and everyone rushed out into the snow without, as far as I could see, paying a farthing to the good woman of the house. But no one stood any chance, and when I got out at the door the train had travelled a hundred yards. The snow was a foot deep, and nothing short of a pair of skis would have enabled anyone to cross it in the time.

Que faire!

I pictured to myself the train arriving at Sevastopol without passengers or guards, and I wondered what would happen to all the unclaimed wraps and bags, and how many roubles it would cost to get them out of the lost property office. I could afford to smile. Most of my property was already lost. Among the other passengers there was consternation. They were like a pack of frightened children, whispering in awe-stricken whispers. Two men insisted on telling me their fears—fears of missing their Christmas, fears of exhausting the vodka supply, fears of wolves, fears of freezing, and a fat man, who had fallen in the snow, kept punctuating their remarks with:

"Devil take me! Lord save us!"

There was nothing to be gained by remaining where we were, so I set out along the railway lines with six others who could walk. The next station proved to be about four miles distant, and after three quarters of an hour we came in sight of it. And in sight of the train! We had walked very seriously and solemnly, like convicts marching to the mines. I, for my part, felt like freezing to death. But at the sight of the train we all burst into exclamation. The Russians gesticulated and waved their handkerchiefs. Then suddenly we thought it might start out before we reached it. The Russians began to run in that peculiar way all foreigners run—as if someone were after them. We arrived in time, feeling pleasantly warm.

I thought when the engine-driver had been remonstrated with he would have backed the train to the wayside stopping-place. But no, he said there was no time, and in ten minutes he started us off again. I have never heard how they fared, these unfortunates who were left behind.

Late in the evening I arrived at Lisitchansk, and Nicholas, my London acquaintance, was actually there waiting for me. He had brought a large fur cloak and rugs. A little pony-sledge was at hand. We fitted ourselves in tightly and gave the word to the driver, who whisked us off through the keen air.

In twenty minutes we had climbed up the steep slope to the village and threaded our way through the broad streets to the cottage of my friend.

CHAPTER II

CHRISTMAS IN LITTLE RUSSIA

I

NICHOLAS was twenty-one years of age and was the eldest child. His father, who was the village deacon, was in his prime. Six feet high, broad-shouldered, he was a proper figure of a man. Thick black hair hung down his back. His high-domed forehead and well-formed aquiline nose reminded one of Tennyson. His wife was a short, dear woman, who moved about in little steps—the sort of woman that never wears out, tender and gentle, but, at the same time, strong-bodied and hardy.

The two of them welcomed me to their home, and I felt thrilled with gratitude. Only he who has been out in the wilds, in distress, in strange parts, among alien people, can know the full joy of a return to home. After long travail, after isolation and privation, one's heart is very sensitive to loving, human hands. It was very sweet for me to realise that in the terrible cold, in the wild night, there was a sheltering roof for me, a little sanctuary where accident and misfortune could no further pursue me, a home where a new father and mother awaited me.

The cottage was a very simple one. It was built of pine trunks placed one across another, reticulated at the corners in the style that children build with firewood. It contained three rooms. The partitions were of bright new wood and unadorned. We sat on straight-back wooden chairs at a wooden table, on which no cloth was spread. The sacred picture, the symbol of God in the home, looked down from a cleft in the pine wall.

The family had lately been at prayers, for Christmas Day begins at six o'clock on the 24th of December. Before us, on the table, stood the allegorical dish of dry porridge, eaten in memory of the hay and straw that lay in the manger in which the Child Jesus was laid. Nicholas's little sister, Zhenia, was helping Masha, the servant, to bring in plates and spoons. A huge bowl, full of boiled honey and stewed fruit, was set in the middle of the table, and then mother and father and son and daughter bowed to the sacred picture and crossed themselves, and sat down to the meal.

The inhabitants of Lisitchansk are Little Russians, and all Little Russians sit down to honey and porridge on Christmas Eve. They call the custom *koutia,* and they cherish it as something distinguishing them from Great Russians or White Russians. The deacon explained its significance to me. What he said sounded rather naïve in my ears. The Communion is a death feast; Koutia is in memory of His birth. " It is just a special Communion service," said he, " and it is held only once a year." He explained how each dish represented the manger: First we put porridge in the dish, which was like putting straw in the manger. The mother helped each of us to porridge; she stood for Mary, who would, of course, see that there was plenty of straw, so that it might be soft and warm. Then we each helped ourselves to honey and fruit and that symbolised The Babe. We made a place in the porridge and then poured the honey and fruit in. The fruit stood for the body; the honey stood for the spirit or the blood. " Blood means spirit, when one is speaking of Christ," said the deacon, whom I perceived to be somewhat of a mystic.

Outside the cottage the wind roared and the snow sifted against the window panes. We were all present at the birth of Christ, and had been transported as if by magic to Bethlehem of Christmas night over nineteen centuries ago.

> " It was the winter wild
> While the heaven-born child
> All meanly wrapt in the rude manger lies."

The brightness of the cottage faded into the half light of a stable, where a child lay in a manger among the horses and the oxen. Joseph and Mary were near and I had just arrived, having followed a particular bright

SIBERIA
ST. PETERSBURG
GREAT RUSSIA
R. VOLGA
NIZHNI NOVGOROD
MOSCOW
WHITE RUSSIA
R. DNIEPER
RIVER VOLGA
KHARKOV
LITTLE RUSSIA
LISITCHANSK
ROUMANIA
R. DNIEPER
LAND OF KALMOUKS
BULGARIA
SEA OF AZOV
STEPPES
BLACK SEA
R. TEREK
VLADIKAVKAZ
CASPIAN SEA
CONSTANTINOPLE
TIFLIS
BAKU
TURKEY IN ASIA
PERSIA

RUSSIA

star that for two thousand miles had led me here. Time itself had given birth to a child. My own new tender life lay in a cradle before me.

Koutia remained on the table and guests came and partook of the meal. They might have been the Wise Men, the Kings with gifts of gold, frankincense and myrrh. Nicholas told me that the guests would return home by a different way from that by which they came —in order to escape Herod. Then the deacon took up a guitar and played carols, typifying, whether he intended it or not, the music of the angel hosts.

I think we spent too little of this night in bed. Much was to happen yet. Nicholas proposed a walk. We bowed to the sacred picture and took our leave. The deacon also had to go out. He curled up his long hair and put it under a high fur hat, and then wrapped himself in a purple cloak.

We stepped out along a narrow trench between two banks of snow, waist-high. There were no lights in the village. The snow fell no longer, but a strong wind blew the drift top in our faces. A heaven, distant and black, but radiant with stars, looked down upon us, and upon the white roofs of the village houses and upon the crosses and domes of the church. All was utterly silent.

At the church the deacon left us, and we went on beyond the village. There is an exposed path that leads up to the crest of the ridge, above the River

Donetz. The wind had swept every loose particle of snow away, so that it was smooth as glass and hard as steel, like a well-used toboggan track. The wind behind us fairly took us up by itself, without any effort on our part, and when we reached the summit it began to blow us down on the other side. It blew us off our feet so that we both went rolling down the steep slope to the river, and we did not gain a foothold till we plunged into a huge bank of snow formed by a rock beside the river bed. It was a very amusing experience and we sat down in the snow and laughed. The wind blew as if it considered our mirth ill-timed. We gathered our cloaks about us and cowered from it.

It was a stiff walk home and the wind was appalling. The sound of music came to us as we came round a bend in sight of the village, and presently we saw a group of carol singers carrying what appeared to be a lantern. When we came nearer we found them to be a group of boys carrying a pasteboard star. The centre of the star was clear and a candle was fixed so that the light shone through; I thought at first it was a turnip lantern. When we looked closer we found that there was a picture of Christ in the centre, so that the light shone through the face. The chief boy carried the star and the next to him twirled the points. It was an interesting point that they made no collection; though, I am told, they all got a few coppers on the morrow. It was a very charming representation of the Star of

Bethlehem. It made its whole journey whilst we were getting home, for we saw it finally enter the church, which, it may be supposed, they considered the most fitting place for the star to rest. They were all boys, and on an English Christmas Eve they would doubtless have been asleep, dreaming of Father Christmas and the car of toys drawn by the reindeer. And that reminds me—Father Christmas knows Russia also. We saw stockings hung outside several cottage doors. It apparently is the custom to hang them outside, so Santa Claus has not to solve the problem of coming down the chimney.

Every cottage window had a light and, looking through, we saw abundance of Christmas fare spread upon the tables. At some there were already guests eating and drinking. The three days' feast had commenced. Nicholas and I went indoors and made a meal and went to bed.

II

The succeeding week was an orgy of eating and drinking. I had already spent one Christmas in England and had eaten not less than a big man's share of turkey and plum-pudding, but I was destined to out-do in Russia every table feat that our homely English board had witnessed. On Christmas Day alone I ate and drank, for courtesy, at eight different houses. Nicholas accomplished prodigious feats, and the worthy deacon was as much beyond Nicholas as the latter was beyond me. Let me describe the spread. There were, of course, chicken, turkey and vodka; there was sucking-pig, roasted with little slices of lemon. There were joints of venison and of beef, roast goose, wild duck, fried sturgeon and carp, fat and sweet, but full of bones; caviare, tinned herrings, mushrooms, melons, infusion of fruit and Caucasian wines. The steaming samovar was always on the sideboard, and likewise tumblers of tea, sweetened with jam or sharpened by lemon slices. There were huge loaves of home-baked bread, but no cakes or biscuits, and no puddings. At peasants' houses the fare was commoner, but not less abundant, than at the squires', and it was very difficult to escape from either without making a meal equal to an English lunch.

The Russians are a hospitable nation and, above all things, like to keep open house. On the great feast days everyone is *at home*—and everyone is also out visiting. That is, the women stay at home and superintend the hospitalities and the men go the rounds. At Moscow it is a full-dress function; one drives about the city all day. At Lisitchansk it is less polite and more hearty than in the old capital and one makes no distinction of persons. Nicholas and I went out to the postman, and together with the postman we went to a poor peasant's dwelling, a one-room cottage where a man and his wife and ten children lived and slept. There was a glorious fire and a pot of soup hanging from a hook over it. Very poor people they were, and the children were thin and wretched, but friends had given them extra coal and food and vodka, and it was as gaily Christmas there as anywhere else. We took a snack of their food and detached the man from his family and went away to the oilman's home. We were four now, and it seemed as if we were going to increase like a ball of snow, but we dropped the postman with the oilman. Just at the door, as we left, we met the deacon, who arranged to meet us at the soap factory in the afternoon, and whilst we were talking the farmer of the vodka monopoly came up and insisted on all of us coming to his house at night. He forcibly reminded me of my train adventure, for he was the first very drunk man I had seen in Lisitchansk. From the moment he appeared on the scene to his actual parting he kept up a grotesque step-dance, the *Kamarinsky Moujik,* the deacon said. It seemed to consist chiefly in doing the *splitz.* After leaving him we went home and were just in time to meet the village police, who had come for Christmas drinks. I think they were all at the fifteenth glass of vodka. It was a matter of speculation to me how far they would get before they finally collapsed. I should think the remoter districts of the village were unvisited by these worthies. One of them had been in Siberia. "Ah, brother, you get vodka out there." Klick, he smacked his lips. "There was an Englishman took a glass of Siberian vodka and for two days he was drunk. On the third day he drank a glass of water and that made him drunk again." Klick, he smacked his lips again. "That's what." And he blinked his eyes at me with peculiar assurance.

When the police had tottered out the village musicians came in playing carols. The leader played the violin; he was the choir-master, an elderly man with flashing eyes and long black hair. Behind him were four young men with guitars or balalaikas. Then came a group of boys, perhaps the same as those who had followed the Star of Bethlehem the night before. They played some hymns and then received coppers all round. The elders drank a glass of vodka each, and then their leader, by way of thanks, gave the Ukrainsky National Dance on the violin, and stamped his feet and danced to the music. Nearly everyone in the room was moving legs or body to the music, and when the musicians made a move to go the scene was so lively that one might have thought the fairy fiddler had been present. The music ceased and the choir hurried away. They had to visit every house in the village, and so time was precious to them; they certainly couldn't linger in the deacon's house. I heard afterwards there was one family they didn't visit; these were Baptists, and had celebrated their Christmas a fortnight earlier with the rest of Europe.

We met the deacon at the soap factory and there made a great feast off sucking-pig. A Little-Russian girl induced me to drink half a glass of vodka on condition that she drank the other half. I insisted that her half should be the first, and then I did not resist the bribe. But I don't think her lips allayed the fire. She had the best of the bargain, and the company collapsed with laughter at my expense.

A number of us left the factory to go to the Squire's, and as we tramped through the snow there was a lively discussion as to the grandeur of the spread and the merits of sucking-pig. The Chief of Police was with us, and he was of opinion that Pavel Ivanovitch was getting too deep in debt.

" What of that," said a military officer, " everyone is in debt. 'Not in debt, not decent.' Don't you know the proverb? "

" How fond you seem to be of getting together and eating and singing and dancing," said I. " In England all the people are huddled up close to one another and yet one seldom takes tea with the next-door neighbour even."

The deacon replied:

" You are all like the people of Moscow or Kiev or St Petersburg, I expect. You have forgotten that you are brothers. Money has come between you and money has made you work. You are all gathered together, not out of love, but out of hate. In England *gregariousness*, in Russia *conviviality*."

" Yes, we live together," said the Chief of Police; " you die together."

" You have your pogroms," I retorted, and everyone looked very grave, for they were all staunch supporters of the Tsar.

" The vine is better for the cutting," said the deacon, softly.

" But surely you do not approve of shedding blood, you do not think it Christian to fight your enemies? "

" We do not strike them. They are cursed by God, and when they are struck it is by Him. But it is not a matter for argument. You have come to see Russia, you look about, and you will find happiness wherever you go. We are all happy, even the Jews, who are only here to make money out of us. Then, if we are happy you must not object to our Government."

" But are you really happy? In nine out of every ten provinces you will have famine before the winter is over, and yet you are all wasting your stores by Christmas luxuriance. All these poor people who are gorging themselves to-day will be pinched with hunger to-morrow."

" He who taketh thought for the morrow is a Jew," said the officer, and so ended the conversation by flooding it with laughter. Everyone laughed, and I think everyone thought we had been getting too serious.

The Squire was the occupant of a grand old house with many spacious rooms and walls a yard thick. His dining-table, about twenty feet long, was heaped up with cold meats and bottles of wine. We were fortunate enough to escape with a plate of turkey and a glass of port each.

As we came home in the dusk we saw a lover and his lass who had just plighted their troth. The deacon insisted on their coming with us. "How was it done?" I asked.

"Oh, she says 'What is your name?'; he replies, 'Foma'; she rejoins, 'Foma is my husband's name.' They are very fond of one another and arranged it of course. It is a custom to plight troth on Christmas Day."

A few days later I was at the girl's house and part of the betrothal ritual was concluded. There were about fourteen of us in one room awaiting the ceremony. Presently a knock came at the door, and the starosta, the old man of the village, entered, and with him the bridegroom. They carried loaves of bread in their hands. The starosta commenced a recitation in a singsong voice. It ran something like this:

"We are German people, come from Turkey. We are hunters, good fellows. There was a time once in our country when we saw strange foot-prints in the snow, and my friend the prince here saw them, and we thought they might be a fox's or a marten's footprints, or it might be those of a beautiful girl. We hunters, we good fellows, are determined not to rest till we have found the animal. We have been in all cities from Germany to Turkey, and have sought for this fox, this marten or this princess, and at last we have seen the same strange foot-prints in the snow again, here by your court. And we have come in. Come, let us take her, the beautiful princess, for we see her in front of us—or can it be you would keep her till she grows a little older?"

Then the father made a speech in the same style, asking the name and lineage of the proud prince who sued for his daughter's hand. Then, after considerable hesitation, both parties came to agreement, and the starosta leading the young man forward, and the father bringing the girl to him, the hands of the loving pair were joined and blessing was given. The rest of the evening was given over to carouse.

But to return to Christmas Day. We spent the night at the house of the farmer of the vodka monopoly. When we met the host he was dancing, and when we said good-night he was still dancing, and he had been dancing all the time. Beyond food there was no real entertainment. A young man played the guitar for four or five hours, and played the same tune the whole time. We had two dinners and two teas. At the second dinner the fifth course was roast sturgeon. I protested that I couldn't eat any more.

"Don't you think you could make all the other things squeeze up just a little and make room?" said the hostess.

"It's the Chief of Police," said the deacon.

" What is? "

" Why, the sturgeon! Don't you know the story of Gogol? The church was packed full of people, so that not a single person more could find room. Then the Chief of Police came and couldn't get in. But the priest called out to the people to make room, and then everyone moved up just a little bit closer. So they managed to squeeze the Chief of Police in. Now this sturgeon is the Chief of Police, and you must make the other things move up."

CHAPTER III

MUMMERS AT A COUNTRY HOUSE

ON St Stephen's Day we drove in sledges to a country house. I feasted my eyes on a wonderful sight — high trees standing between the white ground and the great sun, and casting strange shadows on the whitest snow, and between the shadows a thousand living sparkles literally shot flames from the glistening snow. I had never seen anything like it before; it was very beautiful. We left the forest and passed over a vast plain of tumbled snow. There was snow everywhere as far as eye could see. The sky above was deep glowing blue; the horizon lines a nascent grey darkness. One looked out upon an enchanted ocean of snow; the wind had wreathed it fantastically in crested waves, or left it gently dimpled like the sands of the seashore. Wave behind wave glistened and sparkled to the horizon, and a gentle breeze raised a snow spray from a thousand crests. The snow scud fled from wave to wave. Yes, it was very beautiful and new, and the world seemed very broad and full of peace. I felt it a privilege to exist in the presence of such beauty. It was my name-day, and it seemed as if there were a special significance in all the beauty which lay about me. Pure flame colours were about me as the glistening white robe of a candidate, to whom new mysteries are to be revealed.

The road was hard-beaten snow, a series of frozen cart ruts. The horses scampered ahead and the sledges shot after them. The sledge slipped over the snow like a boat over the reeds of a river. The red-faced driver sat immobile in his seat. We lay back in the sledges and took advantage of every inch of fur and rug. The runners were very low, and we could have touched the snow as we passed. Sometimes we rushed into a drift, and the snow would rise in a splash over us. And wasn't it cold! My feet became like ice.

Our new host was a Count Yamschin, owner of a large estate in the Government of Ekaterinoslav. We arrived at his house in the afternoon, and I heard the deacon give orders to the sledge-drivers to return for us at midnight.

The house was a large one, the rooms spacious. Like Russian houses in general, it was simply and meagrely furnished. But for the people in them the rooms would have seemed empty. There were no carpets on the floor; only here and there a soft Persian rug. The firelight from the logs blazing on the broad hearth was the only illumination until late in the twilight. One watched the shadows about the high ceiling and in the recesses; animated faces moved into the bright gleam of light or passed into the shade. In a corner darker than the others stood the precious Ikons, the sacred pictures.

There were ten or fifteen people in the room, and we chatted in groups for half an hour. The principal topic of conversation was about a mystery play which was going to be performed in the evening. It was called the *Life of Man*, and everyone had evidently heard much about it before the performance. " You will see," said the deacon, " it is an Ikon play. The Ikon speaks." Presently the eldest son came striding in in jack-boots and besought us to go into the concert-hall. This was apparently part of a separate building, and we had all to wrap ourselves up and step into our goloshes, so as to trip through the shrubbery with no discomfort. It was a large hall and would have easily held all the people of the village. There was a stage curtained off, and in the body of the hall a grand piano. We held an impromptu concert, made up for the most part of songs and recitations in the Little Russian language. Little Russian is to Russian what broad Scotch is to English. I met a student who knew many long speeches from Shakespeare by heart, but Shakespeare in Russian translation. Shakespeare is a compulsory subject in most Russian colleges, and students have, on the whole, as good a knowledge of it as English people have. The young man professed to be extremely enthusiastic over the *Life of Man*, which was an expansion of Shakespeare's thought:

> "All the world's a stage,
> And all the men and women merely players."

"Do you believe in God?" asked the student, abruptly.

"Yes," I said. "I use the word God and mean something by it."

"You are old-fashioned." He laughed. "We don't believe in God, we students; we are all atheists. You're coming to Moscow, you'll see. We don't believe in anything except Man. We have given too much time to God already; it's high time we turned our attention to Man. Is it possible you have not yet heard that God is dead? Why, where have you been?"

"I see you have been reading Nietzsche," I remarked with a smile.

He looked at me with annoyance. "The English also read Nietzsche?"

I assented.

"Well," he went on, "we've got God on the stage, you'll see. We don't call him God, but it's God all the same. We call him the old man in grey. We had to do that so as to smuggle him past the censor. The censor, you know, has just stopped Oscar Wilde's *Salome*, not because it's indecent, but because it deals with a biblical subject. I think we've got a better censor than yours, however; he has licensed *Ghosts* and *Mrs Warren's Profession*, and it's perfectly easy to manage him."

"What did the deacon mean when he said the Ikon speaks?"

"Oh, that is his way of looking at it. The huge figure in grey, which you will see, is really meant for God. God gives the play for the benefit of mankind. God speaks the opening words. He shows the life of one man and says it is a typical life, and *that* is man's life upon this earth, *that* and neither more nor less. During all the five acts God stands in a dark corner like an Ikon; he is visible to the audience as a God, but the actors on the stage behave, for the most part, as if it were only a sacred picture. God holds a candle, and as the play gets older the candle gradually burns lower and lower until, when Man dies, it finally expires. To Man on the stage this candle is only visible as the little lamp burning before the Ikon. He makes plans, he succeeds, he fails, he prays or curses, he is trivial or serious, and all the while the candle representing his life burns lower and nothing can stop the wasting of the wax."

At this point Miss Yamschin came and called us all back to dinner. So we all trooped back to the room where the log fire gleamed. Three or four paraffin lamps were now lit, and a pleasant light was diffused through their green shades. An uncle of Nicholas's had arrived, a station-master from a village ten versts away on a by-line. He waited impatiently while the deacon explained who I was, and then transfixed me with this question:

"Who lost the Japanese War—the Russian Government or the people?"

"The Government, of course," I replied. Whereupon he unexpectedly flung his arms round my neck and kissed me on both cheeks.

"If I had had charge of the war, whew!" he whistled. "D'you see the palm of my hand there; now, there's the Japanese Army." Puff, he puffed out his cheeks with air and blew the Japanese Army off his palm and off the face of the earth. He winked at me with assurance. "That's what I'd do." He tapped his head and his chest and said knowingly: "Do you see these, ah-ha, pure Russian, they are."

"Speak to me in English," he went on. "I learned English at school, but I've forgotten—'Not a drum was heard, not a funeral note'—eh? D'ye know that?"

When we got to table the uncle made a long speech, wishing prosperity and happiness to the young Englishman who had come out to Russia to make his fortune. England was the greatest country in the world, next to Russia. If the English soldiers would give up rum and take to vodka they would be the greatest soldiers in the world. When we had all drunk that toast he proposed another, hoping I might find a beautiful Russian girl to love. The count was what we should call a good sort in England. He let everyone do exactly as he pleased, except in the matter of wine, to which no refusals were accepted. It was an uproarious dinner-table; not only the young men, but the girls joined in the conviviality. I was lionised. They drank eleven healths to me all round; it was a matter of wonder what the next plea would be, but the uncle's brain was very fertile. I counted that in all I drank twenty-six glasses of wine that day, and yet when I had been in England I was not quite sure whether I was a teetotaller or not. I was finally persuaded to make a speech in Russian, in which my Russian gave way, and I was forced to conclude in English. I managed to propose the host's health, and that was the best thing I could have done. Approbation was uproarious.

When, at last, the dinner was over, we filed into the concert-hall to see the *Life of Man* performed. My student companion was evidently one of the actors, since I looked to resume our conversation, but he was nowhere to be found. The drama was one of Leonid Andrief's, a new Russian author, whose works have been making him a great name in Russia during the last five years. The *Life of Man* was produced in the Theatre of Art, Moscow, said to be the greatest theatre in the world. It has made a great impression in Russia;

I have come across it everywhere in my wanderings, even in the most unlikely places. Its words and its characters have become so familiar to the public that one scarcely opens a paper without finding references to it. It has been the inspiration of thousands of cartoonists.

It was true, as the student had said, God, as it were, gave the play. The words of the prologue were among the most impressive I have ever heard, and spoken as they were in dreadful sepulchral tones by a figure who, at least, stood for God, they are fixed indelibly in my memory. My programme said, "*Prologue : Someone in the greyness speaks of the life of a Man.*" As the Prologue is a summary of the play, I shall give it. Picture a perfectly dark stage, and in the darkness a figure darker than the darkness itself, enigmatical, immense.

"*Behold and listen,*" it said, "*ye people, come hither for amusement and laughter. There passes before you the life of a Man—darkness in the beginning, darkness at the end of it. Hitherto not existent, buried in the boundless time, unthought of, unfelt, known by none ; he secretly oversteps the bounds of nonentity, and with a cry announces the beginning of his little life. In the night of nothingness, a lamp casts a gleam, lit by an unseen hand —it is the life of Man. Look upon the flame of it—the life of a Man.*

"*When he is born he takes the form and name of man and in all things becomes like other people already living upon the earth. And the cruel destiny of these becomes his destiny, and his cruel destiny the destiny of all people. Irresistibly yoked to time he unfailingly approaches all the steps of Man's life, from the lower to the higher, from the higher to the lower. By sight limited, he will never foresee the next steps for which he raises his tender feet; by knowledge limited, he will never know what the coming day will bring him, the coming hour—minute. And in his blind ignorance, languishing through foreboding, agitated by hopes, he submissively completes the circle of an iron decree.*

" Behold him—a happy young man. Look how brightly the candle burns! The icy wind of the limitless sky cannot disturb, or in the slightest deflect the movement of the flame. Radiantly and brightly burns the candle. But the wax diminishes with the burning. The wax diminishes.

" Behold him—a happy husband and father. But, look how dully and strangely the candle-light glimmers, as if its yellowed flame were withering, trembling from the cold and hiding itself. And the wax is wasting, following the burning. The wax is wasting.

" Behold him—an old man, sickly and weak. Already the steps of life are ending, and a black chasm is in the place of them—but, spite of that, his trembling feet are drawn forwards. Bending towards the earth, the flame, now blue, droops powerlessly, trembles and falls, trembles and falls—and slowly expires.

" So Man will die. Coming out of the night he will

return to the night and vanish without traces into the boundless time, unthought of, unfelt, known by none. And I, then, named by all He, remain the true fellow-traveller of Man in all the days of his life, in all his ways. Unseen by Man and near him, I shall be unfailingly beside him when he wakes and when he sleeps, when he prays or when he curses. In the hours of pleasure when he breathes freely and bravely, in the hours of despondency and grief, when the languor of death darkens his soul and the blood grows cold about his heart, in the hours of victory and of defeat, in the hours of the great struggle with the inevitable, I shall be with him. I shall be with him.

"*And you come hither for amusement, you, the devoted of death, behold and listen. With this far-off and phantasmal figure there unfolds itself to your gaze, with its sorrows and its joys, the quickly passing life of Man.*"

The voice from the grey figure ceased, and in the dark a curtain came down over the scene.

The play was as foreshadowed. In the first act a Man is born, in the second he is a struggling young man, in the third he is a successful man, in the fourth he is in decline, and in the fifth he dies. The figure in grey appears at the birth of Man, and is visible to the audience throughout the five acts. He holds a burning candle, which is radiantly bright in Act iii., but which gutters out at the end of Act v. Fates, old women, nornas, are in attendance at the birth, and they are again in attendance at death.

The story is delicately told and affecting. Man is young and happy and the obstacles in his life are only means of happiness; he succeeds and all the world does homage to him; he passes the prime of life and new obstacles appear, and these serve only to bring him unhappiness; he is brought low and he dies.

The actor who played Man's part was a robust, handsome man with flashing eyes and long hair. Whilst he played the young Man he was careless, brave, free, and when he became old he was dignified, proud and obstinate. His destiny, it seemed to me, was comprised between a challenge and a curse. In his despair in Act ii., when life seemed a feast to which he was not bidden, he was stung to anger and defiance against Fate. He turned to where the ikon stood and flung a challenge at the Unknown.

" *—Hi you! you there! what d'you call yourself? Fate, devil or life, there's my glove; I'll fight you! Wretched, poor-spirited folk curse themselves before your enigmatical power: thy stone face moves them to terror, in thy silence they hear the beginning of calamities and their own terrible ruin. But I am brave and strong and I challenge you to battle. With bright swords, with sounding shields, we will fall at one another's heads with blows at which the earth will tremble. Hi! Come out and fight.*

" *To thy ominous slow movement I shall oppose my living, vigilant strength; to thy gloom my gay sounding laugh! Hi! Take that blow, ward it off if you can! Your brow is stone, your reason lost. I throw into it the red-hot shot of my bright sense; you have a heart of stone that has lost all pity, give way! I shall pour into it the burning poison of my rebellious cries! By the black cloud of thy fierce anger the sun is obscured; we shall light up the gloom with dreams! Hi! Take that!*

" Conquering, I will sing songs which all the world will cheer; silently falling under thy blow, my only thought shall be of rising again to battle! There is a weak place in my armour, I know it. But, covered with wounds, the ruby blood flowing, I shall yet gather strength to cry—and even then, thou evil enemy of Man, I shall overcome Thee. And, dying on the field of battle, as the brave die, with one loud amen I shall annul thy blind pleasure! I have conquered, I have conquered my wicked enemy; not even in my last breath do I acknowledge his power. Hi, there! Hi! Come out and fight! With bright swords, with sounding shields, we shall fall at one another with blows at which the earth will tremble! Hi! Come out and fight!"

The deacon, the count, his daughters, the tenants and guests all looked on with breathless interest. We of the audience knew that which Man on the stage knew not. We knew that even whilst he was raging against Fate his fortune was being achieved and his success assured by two men in a motor-car who were driving about the town, unable to find Man's wretched dwelling.

Success came and it vanished. "Vanity of vanities," saith the preacher; so I thought, but Man cursed. He pointed with outstretched arm as if in delirium at the stone face of the ikon and shrieked:

"*I curse Thee and all Thou gavest me. I curse the day on which I was born and the day when I shall die. I curse all my life, its pleasures and pains, I curse myself! I curse my eyes, my hearing, my tongue, I curse my heart, my head—and everything I throw again into Thy stern face, senseless Fate. Cursed, cursed for ever! And with the curse I overcome Thee. What remains that Thou canst do with me? Hurl me to the ground, hurl, I shall laugh and shout 'I curse Thee!' With the pincers of Death stop my mouth; with my last sense I shall cry into Thy ass's ears, 'I curse Thee, I curse Thee.' Take my dead body, nibble it, like a dog, carry it away into the darkness—I am not in it, I am vanished away, but vanished, repeating, 'I curse Thee, I curse Thee.' Through the head of the woman thou hast insulted, through the body of the child thou hast killed—I send to Thee the Curse of Man.*"

The dreadful grey figure stood unmoved, silent as the Sphinx. Only the flame of the candle in its hand wavered as if the wind blew it. All of us in the audience shuddered, and the uncle who had become very solemn suddenly began to sob.

Act v. was a dance of drunkards and fates in a cellar tavern, dark, dirty, fearful. The dreadful, implacable figure in grey stood far in the darkest corner, and near him, on a bench, sat Man breathing out his last. The uncle astonished me, and for the moment almost terrified me by crying out in English:

"Out, out, brief candle."

Truly, it is strange what quantities of English literature one finds in even remote places in Russia.

But to return, Man died, and none too soon, and the candle went out. There was no cheering of the actors, though they were warmly congratulated by the count later on. We all left the little theatre and went back to supper.

At midnight the sledges came. The uncle insisted on our going home with him. So we went to his railway station. Thus ended our night with the mummers at Count Yamschin's country house.

IV

AT UNCLE'S

UNCLE was station-master of a little place called Rubezhniya, a village of ten families. Rubezhniya is on the edge of a great forest, though, I think, that in Russia they call it a little wood. It extends a few hundred miles, but then there is a forest in Russia where a squirrel might travel straight on eastward four thousand miles, going from branch to branch and never touching earth once. Rubezhniya is also on the black land, and its peasants have money in the autumn, though, it may be remarked, there is never any left by the time winter approaches. Surplus money, unfortunately, finds its way quickly to the exchequer of an unthrifty Government and to the pockets of the farmer of the vodka monopoly.

There are no savings banks in Russia and no wives' stockings. Ivan Ivanovitch lives hand to mouth; what he earns he spends, and when he earns nothing he gets food from the man next door, or rather next field—for, except in towns, there is no next door, and in the villages there is seldom anything so regular as a road. Rubezhniya was supposed to be suffering from famine and the whole district to be in want of relief; I was therefore interested to see whether Christmas fare was less plentiful there than in Lisitchansk.

Uncle locked us in the first-class waiting-room and bade us undress and be comfortable as if at home. The mother and Zhenia he took to his own small lodging. Once in later days, when I begged hospitality of a "pope," he put me in the church, and on another occasion, when I went to see a police-officer, he asked me if I would mind sleeping in a cell as he was full up at home. In some respects Russians are Spartans.

We did undress *a little* and turned out the lamp. The room was dark save for the little light that burned before the Ikon, and there was silence. We composed ourselves to sleep, but after about half an hour came the heavy rumble of a train. We heard steps on the platform, the soft crunching sound of someone walking through crisp snow. Two bells sounded. "The train waits five minutes here," whispered the deacon, gruffly.

Suddenly a key turned in our door and a hoarse voice exclaimed:

"Devil take it, where's the light? I've brought a little friend."

It was Uncle again. I am sure we all cursed a little inwardly. But he found his way to the lamp and lit it. The first thing I noticed was a red parcel on the table. The parcel turned out to be a baby.

"A little friend I've brought," said Uncle, apologetically.

"Where'd ye find it?" asked Nicholas.

It was a baby in a sack of red quilted flannel. Uncle picked it up by the flap of the sack and let it dangle from his thumb and forefinger in a way to cause a mother's heart to tremble.

"Mine," he said.

"A girl or a boy?" I asked.

"His name is Tarass, Tarass Bulba, eh?" He brought the baby to me and sat down on my legs, for I had not got up from the park seat on which I was resting.

"Where is his mother?" I asked. He put his finger to his lips.

"Asleep; say nothing. My little cossack, *there's* an arm for you," said he, taking a chubby little limb from its cosy resting-place, whereupon he proceeded to undress the child for our edification. But just as he was concluding that delicate operation a man in a goat-skin hat and jacket burst into the waiting-room, and a couple of porters and three third-class passengers.

"Outside, cut-throats," said Uncle, pulling out a pistol from his belt. The porters and the passengers fled. But the man in the goat-skin jacket held up his arms as if Uncle had cried "Hands up!" and from the moment he burst in he had kept saying "Water!" as if he was demented or the train was on fire.

" Water, water, water! " Uncle put up his pistol in his belt again.

" More softly," he whispered. " You want water? You'll get no water here; vodka plenty, but water none."

I came to the conclusion it must be another comic engine-driver. He protested by Mary in heaven that they could not go on without water.

" Won't vodka do? "

The engine-driver smiled evasively as much as to say, " You are pleased to be funny, but this is a serious matter." Then the baby began to scream.

" Devil take it," said Uncle. " Clear out. There *is* no water I tell you. Wait for a luggage train to push you to the next station or go to the devil." At this point a passenger came in, an aged moujik with long white hair.

" God bless all here," said the moujik.

" What *is* the matter? "

" The devil is in our midst! " He crossed himself and bowed to the Ikon. " Lord have mercy upon us, for an unclean spirit has come out of the forest! "

" Colour of his eyes? " asked Nicholas, maliciously.

" Red, like fire, your Excellency. An unclean spirit has come out of the forest and entered into the body of Pavel Fedoritch."

" He means a man in the train has gone mad," said Nicholas. " That comes of running your trains so fearfully fast and using up all your water."

The engine-driver protested mildly and then stared at the baby, who was yelling as if Satan had entered into it as well as into Pavel Fedoritch.

" Lord God, preserve us," said the engine-driver, and crossed himself feverishly.

" A man has gone mad," said Uncle. " Very well, take him to the police station and ask them to cut his head off; and now *outside* all those who haven't got first-class tickets! "

He rose to push them all out but suddenly gave way to one mightier than he. A burly woman in a red petticoat pushed through the little crowd assembled at the doorway, and levelled abuse to right and to left till she got right in and snatched up the baby. It was Auntie. It was Uncle's wife, and Uncle subsided and Auntie scolded them all for disturbing our rest and cleared the room. Then she sat on the table and quieted the child and told us what a good-for-nothing her husband was. Poor Uncle! He sat meekly by and listened. He evidently felt very sorrowful.

Then she left us and the train went out, without water and without discharging the unclean spirit, I believe, and we were left with Uncle, who insisted on our coming to the bar and making a meal. After that, at about 5.30 a.m., we retired to the waiting-room, there to glean what sleep we might in the three hours that were left to us.

From utter weariness I could have slept all day, but

Uncle had no mercy. We were obliged to wake up at seven. The door opened again, and a very ragged and dirty young man lit the gas. He sprinkled some water on the floor and swished a mop over it. He had no boots or stockings on, but there were pieces of hard sheep-skin on the soles of his feet, and with these he polished the floor, dancing and stamping, rubbing and smoothing. Russian floors are generally of tessellated wood and are polished in this manner. At eight we had to wash and dress and go up to Uncle's for breakfast.

The deacon proposed to go to Lisitchansk directly after breakfast. Uncle said we must have dinner first, and then he would come also. I wanted to stay and look around, so I proposed that Nicholas and I remain with Uncle, and that the old folks and Zhenia might go back if they wanted to and we would come on in the afternoon. They agreed. Father, mother and daughter went off in one sledge, Zhenia sitting on her father's knee, and we strolled away to the forest—" to shoot wolves," Uncle said.

We passed through the village, a collection of mud huts and pine izbas, all much poorer than Lisitchansk.

" Come and spend the summer here," said Uncle.

" No, he's coming to Lisitchansk," said Nicholas.

" It doesn't look very tempting," I replied.

" Oh, don't judge by the present," said Uncle· " we are all sleeping like bears in their holes. We don't really wake up till the spring."

"Yes, like bears," said Nicholas. "Every nation tends to take the characteristics of the animals amongst which it lives; the Russians are like bears, the Indians are like snakes, the Irish like pigs, the Australians like kangaroos, the English like cows."

"Nonsense," said Uncle; "the Russians are like eagles, the English like lions—eh?"

I agreed—the Russians were as much like eagles as the English like lions.

"There aren't any eagles in Russia except in the Caucasus," said Nicholas.

"Yes, that's the place to go to, the Caucasus, full of bears," said Uncle.

I laughed and pointed out that I was going to Moscow first, there to finish the winter. The summer was a long way off and I could foresee nothing. But it was probably during this talk that it first occurred to me to go to the Caucasus and tramp the mountains there. Moscow, however, was the idea that forced itself upon my consideration, for as soon as this Little-Russian visit was completed I intended to go thither.

In the forest we met the village moujiks, all engaged in cutting timber and loading sledges, and Uncle amused himself and us by feats of log-lifting. He was very proud of his strength.

At dinner-time his wife forbade him to go to Lisitchansk, and he, after some protest about his promises, obeyed her. The Christmas festival was evidently

A RUSSIAN STREET SCENE

A CAUCASIAN CHIEF

ending. The feasting and revelry of the past three days was like a gay dream from which we were awaking, awaking into a grey, ordinary world.

" If you go to the Caucasus come *via* Rubezhniya," said Uncle, as he kissed us in the sledge and bade us good-bye.

CHAPTER V

AMONG MOSCOW STUDENTS

AT Kharkov, on my return journey, I recovered half of my lost luggage; the other half, a box full of books and papers, had not turned up: neither by bribes nor by words could it be found. We spent a whole day searching the Customs House, but failed to find any trace of it. I learned afterwards that it had been left behind at Ostend, through the negligence of a porter there. The loss of this box was a matter of sorrow. All through the winter I felt the loss of it. It was only in April, after immense correspondence, that I recovered it, and then it was no use since I had made up my mind to spend the summer on the mountains.

The loss of my overcoat and of my box had evidently made a deep impression on Nicholas. He was determined he should lose none of his things. We were travelling together all the way to Moscow. He was going to be a student at the University, and he hoped to share lodgings with me. Our journey took three days. Nicholas's luggage consisted of nine heavy portmanteaux and boxes. This luggage was a matter of amazement to myself, my fellow-travellers and the porters. Surely no one ever before started from a pine cottage with such an accumulation. How Nicholas came by it all will always be an interesting page in his life history.

A year ago, Nicholas had been studying in Moscow and supporting himself by giving lessons in English, music and mathematics. Of all his studies the favourite was English; and in English he excelled. His professor regarded him as a lad of promise, and advised him to go for a season to England and learn to speak the language. Nicholas was of an adventurous spirit and the advice pleased him. He saved a few pounds and set off for England. First he went home and told the deacon and his mother. They were astonished beyond words. They did not, however, forbid the journey; they blessed him and bade him farewell, commending him to the saints. His mother kissed the little Ikon which hung round his neck, and looked her son in the eyes with that peculiar expression of faith which is part of the In-itself of life. Zhenia kissed him good-bye, and the young adventurer went out into the wide world into the new lands. His route was interesting, being the route which so many poor emigrants were taking at that time, lured by the stories of fabulous wages in England, America and Canada. He took steamer at Ekaterinoslav and came leisurely up the Dneiper to Kiev, the busy city generally spoken of as ancient, though new as Paris and swirling with electric cars. From Kiev he went by train; third-class to the Konigsberg frontier and thence across Germany, fourth-class to Hamburg. Does the reader know a fourth-class emigrant train? It is a series of cattle-trucks for human beings, and indeed the occupants behave more like animals than human beings. Anything more filthy, indecent and odious than the condition of a Jews' train can scarcely be imagined. I think Nicholas felt very sick and weary before he got to Hamburg. But it was cheap travelling. I think his whole fare, from Lisitchansk to London, cost less than two pounds ten.

He was a brave boy. I imagine his arrival in London at the dreary docks, his first view of our appallingly large, dreary city. He did not see the fairy-tale which it is the fashion to see in London. It was a friendless desert, a place where everyone was so poor that it took all one's time to look after oneself. He wandered about and lost himself, if, indeed, it were possible to lose himself, since he was already lost when he arrived that early May morning. There was one thing to do: he had a Russian's address in his pocket, the address of a Russian in London. By dint of asking a new policeman at each turning he found his way to Russell Square.

Lucky boy! He fell on his feet in Bloomsbury in the Russian colony there. Russians are very kind to one another, and it would be difficult not to be kind to

Nicholas; he is handsome, witty, musical. One introduced him to another all the way round, and he found occupation easily, giving lessons once more in English, music and mathematics. It was in this first period that he met me. I had written to the Russian Consul asking if he would recommend me a Russian who would be willing to give me lessons in the Russian language. He indicated a certain M. Voronofsky, who referred me to Nicholas. So I came to know him. He was surely the most affectionate teacher I ever had, and most prodigal he was in Russian conversation. He gave me hours beyond the stipulated time of my lesson, and would walk arm-in-arm with me up and down the Strand, protesting his affection and heaping endearments upon me in a way that made me fancy what it is like to be a girl. I was, however, in some respects unlucky in my teachers; as fast as I got one he disappeared and was next heard of in Barrow-in-Furness. The reason for this lay in the fact that Messrs Vickers Maxim had obtained a contract to build a portion of the new Russian fleet. Besides an immense amount of correspondence with the Russian Admiralty, all plans, specifications and directions were in Russian, and in technical Russian at that. Consequently a large Russian staff was required at Barrow, and almost anyone who applied was accepted at once. I told Nicholas of this, he applied and was accepted. So for the time I lost him. He worked three months, literally grinding, doing twelve hours' work a day. He found out what it was to be utilised in the English machine. I think he did not like it, and it was only the joy of earning a pile of money that kept him at it. He made eighty pounds in three months, which wasn't bad for a youngster. But at the end of that time a wave of home-sickness overtook him. A letter from home said his father was unwell; he interpreted it to mean his father was dying, packed up his things and left the country. He had arrived in London with one black box, he went away with—nine heavy portmanteaux and trunks. He said to me, when he came back from Barrow, "I want to buy all sorts of things; if I don't buy them now I shall never buy them again; I shall never have the money." Now, to a Russian, England is a paradise of cheap clothes. Living is dear but clothes are dirt cheap. In Russia only my lord wears a collar or uses a handkerchief; an English suit costs five pounds at least, English shirts cost six or seven shillings each. Nicholas bought a wardrobe of suits and fancy waistcoats, hats, boots, umbrellas, ties. Such ties he bought that at several Lisitchansk parties he had to undress partially so as to satisfy the curiosity of his friends. He bought patent Mikado braces, the like had never been seen in Little Russia. He bought Zhenia a hat, and his father a smoking jacket, and his mother a shawl. He bought reams of delicately-tinted notepaper and envelopes, at which, since those days, numberless fair Russian girls have gazed; though "fairer than the paper writ on was the fair hand that writ." I took him into Straker's one day to help him to make some purchases; we spent half an hour selecting shades of sealing-wax. Well, you can be sure that by the time he finished his packing there was not much space left in those nine boxes and bags. I saw him off at Liverpool Street Stati n. He went home *via* the Hook of Holland and in grand style. It was a strange contrast to his arrival five months before.

Of course he found his father very well when he came to Lisitchansk, and he spent a very gay autumn there. He was the prodigal come home, but with the fatted calf under his arm. It was very glorious for him. Yet from the point of view of material prosperity his return was a mistake. The tide which leads to fortune had been at the full for him in London. He had wilfully neglected it.

Success turned his head a little. He lived on glory for a month or two, and then he heard that I was coming to Russia and he invited me to his home. His mind became full of plans: he would go to Canada, he would go to England again, or to Chicago. The first step, however, towards the realisation of these or any other schemes was to obtain money. He had spent all his English earnings.

I came and stated my intention of going to Moscow. Nicholas discovered that Moscow was the best place for him. He would come with me and learn more

English, and he would study for his degree and pay for his living and his fees by giving lessons.

He ought to have gone straight to Moscow in the autumn, for the University year commences in September, and the person who starts in January finds himself hardly circumstanced in many ways. For one thing, it is very difficult to earn money by teaching. It is a custom in Russian families of the middle and upper classes to employ what are known as *repetitors.* A *repetitor* is a University student who comes each night to hear the lessons in the family. The boys and girls go to school in the morning, they prepare their home-lessons in the afternoon, and in the evening and at night they say them over to *repetitors.* A student of ability has a fair chance of earning eight or ten pounds a month by this, and there is scarcely a student in Moscow who does not glean two or three pounds at least by it. But practically the whole of this teaching is arranged in September or October, at the commencement of the session, for all schools work in harmony with the University and have the same terms and vacations. So Nicholas was coming out of time. In truth, neither his prospect nor mine would have tempted an investor. But neither of us understood the position, and each relied a little on the other. Nicholas thought my journalism would bring me in untold wealth, and I thought I might be able to get some teaching through him. So the blind led the blind.

At Moscow we were met by Shura, a Little-Russian friend of Nicholas; Alexander Sergayef was his name in full, though he was called Shura or Sasha for short. He was a philological student and shared rooms with a Greek in the Kislovka. The three of us drove to a lodging-house at Candlemas Gate (Sretinka Vorota), and the portmanteaux and boxes followed behind on a dray.

The lodging-house goes by the name of "Samarkand," which is printed on a disreputable blue board which hangs outside. It is a dirty establishment like five hundred of its kind in the city. The lodgers are chiefly clerks and students, and, before the Governor stepped in with new regulations, card-sharpers and gamblers. One commonly collided with queer characters on the stairs—beggars, spies, touts; girls in gay hats hung on the banisters, smoked cigarettes, flirted with the door-keeper and the students. In front the building looked down upon a beer-tavern; behind it stood the Candlemas Monastery, a church of cheese-yellow and bottle-green, surrounded by seven purple domes. On each dome was a gilt cross, and on the cross fat crows often perched. We took a room on the third floor; it cost two pounds a month—a very cheap price for Moscow. It was an advantage to us to be nearer the sky than the street; we had light and air and view. We had more cold, perhaps, but that was a minor matter. No town houses have fire-places except rich mansions built in the English style, but there is excellent steam-heating, and even on the coldest days we never felt a chill, though we were high up and exposed to the wind. For me, indeed, it was a most pleasant experience to be able to turn out of bed in the morning and feel the room as warm as it was when I went to bed. Russian houses, even the poorest, are more comfortable in winter than the English.

Our room was a large one, having five chairs and three rickety little tables, besides a couple of couches and two beds. In a grey corner an Ikon of the Virgin hung. I, for my part, had my own Ikon, a print of Millet's " Angelus," which I placed in front of my table. It made even this poor room a living, breathing home. It was my reminder of England. Since those days when I lived at Samarkand it has become very sacred to me.

We were very poor. I think when I had bought an overcoat and Nicholas had paid his fees we had just three pounds between us. We lived on black bread, milk and fried pork. I wrote my articles, he went and hawked about the town for lessons.

Among the precious things in the capacious pockets that overcoat which was stolen was a book on the *Russian Peasant*. This had been given me by a London editor who let me have " a shot at reviewing it." I grieved not a little that this had been lost before I had read it thoroughly. I had only glanced through it in the train. My loss did not deter me from writing the article, however. What was my surprise when in the second week of my stay at Moscow, almost by return of post, the editor wrote, "Review excellent, fire away, try something else." I felt very cheerful and reflected that by mid-February at the latest I should receive my first cheque.

But meanwhile it became apparent that we stood a chance to starve. We were living on an average of less than fourpence a day each. In a note-book, which I kept at that time, I see that on January 14th I spent 5d. on food, on the 15th, 4d. The figures are interesting:—

January 16th	6d.
,, 17th	3d.
,, 18th	4d.
,, 19th	3d.
,, 20th	1d.
,, 21st	5d.
,, 22nd	2d.

and so on.

On the 28th Shura came round to see us, told us his Greek companion had left him, and invited us to come and live with him. Forthwith the three of us, the nine boxes and bags and my luggage, proceeded in sledges to the Kislovka, and we took up our abode in the students' quarter.

The district known as the Kislovka lies at the back of the University. It is an ugly aggregation of lodging-houses. Each lodging-house is composed of students' dens. Some students have rooms to themselves, but for the most part a single one is let to two or three students. Three young men, like ourselves, will sleep, eat, study and receive company in the same room. We had to pay about fourteen shillings a month each, so the arrangement seemed more economical. Then Shura earned about four pounds a month giving lessons, so the financial position was much improved. Then, on the second night after we had been there, Nicholas won fifteen shillings off a Frenchman at cards. Then on February 5th there came a letter to me from a London newspaper enclosing a cheque in respect of a Christmas article I had sent in. It was too late for this Christmas, they would use it next. It was evident we should not starve.

On Saturday Shura had an "At Home" day. We always stayed up all night on Saturdays. In the afternoons we bought rolls and sausage and caviare and tinned herring and cheese to make a spread. About five or six o'clock the guests would arrive—five or six girl students and the same number of men. There were not chairs to go round, so many of them sat on the beds. Then we talked in the way that only Russians can. On the floor lay cigarette-ends, volumes on law and philosophy, dust of past ages, vodka droppings from the last gathering, old clothes, newspapers, picture postcards. The walls were plastered with prints, portraits of members of the Duma, a large newspaper picture of

Tolstoy, cartoons from European papers, etc. My "Angelus" Ikon looked almost sorrowfully upon the scene. There was no real Russian Ikon there. Shura told me he had pitched it out of the window when he came. He didn't believe in God. In the course of the evening one of the students present would read a tale from Tchekhof or Andrief, another would read a few verses from Nadson, their favourite poet. Nicholas would play on the guitar and sing little Russian songs. I would get through a game at chess with someone. Then we would all play some games at forfeit with the girls. The time passed very quickly. One samovar would succeed another until after midnight, and glasses of weak tea circulated till dawn. At last we would take the girls home, and then come back and sleep an hour or two before breakfast. It was a godless way of beginning the Sunday.

Shortly after the first "At Home" I discovered a way in which an Englishman can make a small fortune in Moscow. I put an advertisement in the *Russian Word* to this effect:—

"Young Englishman from London, well-educated, seeks lessons, speaks French and Russian."

The answers to this soon made me the richest of the three in the little room. My lowest price was four shillings a lesson of one hour. An Englishman can get that easily in Moscow. I became a *repetitor*. First I had a French girl to teach, the daughter of a cotton manufacturer. She didn't like me and I lost that lesson after a fortnight, but I got lessons with an engineer, with two German boys and a Russian boy; and a woman engaged me to give a series of lectures on English literature at a girls' college. For the last named I received six shillings a lecture.

Then Nicholas got three pounds a month to coach a boy for his matriculation; we were all thriving.

CHAPTER VI

"LOVE US WHEN WE ARE DIRTY FOR EVERYONE WILL LOVE US WHEN WE ARE CLEAN!"

IN February Moscow was overrun by an epidemic of typhus. It did not spring from the frozen drains so much as from the indigestible black bread which is sold in the poorer parts of the city. On 10th February I gave up black bread for ever; I have not eaten it since—at least not Moscow black bread; Caucasian black bread is another matter. The bread diet had become too much for me. I lay in bed all one day feeling more dead than alive, and the prospect of typhus seemed very real. I recovered, and then substituted porridge and milk for the old diet. I showed Shura and Nicholas how to make this in the Scotch way, and they got very keen on it and showed other students. So I might almost claim to have introduced Scotch porridge to Moscow University. The Russian peasants and poor people in general make a porridge of buck-wheat, *Kasha* they call it, but I am quite sure it is less cheap, less wholesome, and less tasty than oatmeal porridge.

Moscow in winter is remarkable for its poor people,

its labourers, its beggars, its students. Cab-drivers in Moscow take twopence-halfpenny a mile, and I have frequently taken a sledge from Sukareva Tower to the Vindavsky Station for fifteen copecks—4d., a distance of two miles. At the Khitry market one may often see men and women with only one cotton garment between their bodies and the cruel cold. How they live is incomprehensible; they are certainly a different order of being from anything in England. And the beggars! They say there are 50,000 of them. The city belongs to them; if the city rats own the drains, they own the streets. They are, moreover, an essential part of the city; they are in perfect harmony with it; take away the beggars and you would destroy something vital. Some are so old and weather-battered that they make the Kremlin itself look older, and those who lie at the monastery doors are so fearfully pitiable in their decrepitude that they lend power to the churches. Moscow would be a different place without the gaunt giants who hang down upon one and moan for bread; without the little cripples who squirm upon the pavement and scream their wants at the passer-by. To me, though I found them a plague at first, they were a perpetual interest. There were among them some of the strangest people one could expect to meet anywhere: worn-out, yellow-whiskered men with icicles in their beards, limbless trunks of men, abortions of men and women. I saw many nationalities; Letts, Poles, Jews,

Tartars, Tatars, Bohemians, Caucasians, Chinese, Bokharese, specimens of all the peoples who exist under the Russian Eagle. Rich Russians allege that they collect five shillings a day, which is on a par with the tales of wealth amassed by organ-grinders in London. The daily task of each is to obtain twopence—a penny for a pound of black bread, a penny for a bed in a night house. They just about manage this, sometimes getting a little more, sometimes a little less. The surplus goes in vodka.

The question has to be faced by the traveller—What are you going to do with the beggars? I felt the need of a definite policy. At first, when we ourselves were near starving, I said "*No*" consistently, for I hadn't any money. Then when money came I hardened my heart and said, "It is better to be a thief than a beggar: it is more manly. If I give to beggars I make it more profitable to be a beggar; I attract other people to beggary. If I withhold my money I drive some beggars to robbery, and then the police have to deal with them." If the people were properly looked after there would be no need to rob or beg. This was a clear decision, and I held by it rigorously for a long time, till at last I came to the conclusion that it was more unpleasant to refuse some beggars than to give alms. Truly, whether an Englishman gives or gives not he feels he does wrong. Eventually I abandoned my principle and gave when I felt inclined. The Russian has no mental scruples.

He is generally, providentially, ignorant of the science of economics. One fact is evident to him: the beggar is cold and hungry and it is Christian to help him. And the Socialists are too busy over bigger things to define their attitude to the poor wretch whom they deem to be a victim of tyranny. It is a common happening to see a crowd of unfortunate creatures being driven to the police-station by a couple of soldiers. To the democrat that is sufficient evidence of tyranny. Still, I have been told the beggars have nothing to fear from the authorities. The beggar is a holy institution; he keeps down the rate of wages in the factories; he is the pillar of the church, for he continually suggests charity; he is necessary to the Secret Police; where else could they hide their spies?

The beggars have the most extraordinary licence and think nothing of walking in at a back-door and staring at you for a quarter of an hour. It is this licensed insolence that makes him a terror to the nervous Russian, who always considers himself watched by spies. Nicholas appeared to be continually suspecting and dreading spies. On the second day after we arrived at the Samarkand lodging-house he discovered a spy on the same floor, so he said. Often when I was walking with him in the town he would say to me in a whisper, " Slow down and let the man behind us get past." Once we slowed down in vain, and then put on speed in vain· we could not rid ourselves of a beggar who persisted in following us. Nicholas suddenly turned round in terror at a dark corner and clutched hold of the beggar with both hands and shook him. Then it was the beggar's turn to have a fright, but he only asked meekly:

"Why did you do that to me, barin?"

The word "barin," "bar," means a master; it is interesting that the word spelt backwards, *rab*, means a slave. Russians say this is not merely a coincidence.

The different way in which beggars address one would make an interesting study. I remember one night a dreadful amorphous remnant of a man, lying in a currant box outside the Cathedral of St Saviour, addressed me in this fashion:

"Imagine that I am God!"

One seldom, however, hears such a dramatic utterance. Much commoner is lighter banter. I remember a cheeky boy came up to me smiling and certain.

"A copeck, dear count!"

"Haven't got one, your Majesty," I replied.

Many of the beggars have a selection of tales of woe carefully worked up to suit the susceptibilities of different passers-by. Of this kind was an old stalwart whom we, of the Kislovka room, used to patronise. His usual style was:

"I was a soldier at the Turkish War and astonished three generals by my bravery, but now devil a penny will my country give me to keep my old bones together."

But the two girl students who occupied the room next to ours always averred that he told them a yarn about his daughter dying from want of food and his wife in consumption, but never said a word about his exploits.

Nicholas and I dressed ourselves in our worst and went to a night-house one night. At five o'clock in the evening there was a queue like a first night pit-crowd at His Majesty's Theatre in London, a street full of beggars pushing, jostling, shouting and singing. Next door to the doss-house was a tavern, to which every now and then someone unable to oppose temptation would dash to get a glass of vodka. Admission to this house cost one penny. It was rather a fearsome den to go into, and I wonder at ourselves now. I thought we should be too far down the line to get in, but I was mistaken. Everyone was admitted. We passed through a turnstile, and, strange to say, showed no passports. I fancy most of the beggars are passportless. A policeman stood at the door and scrutinised the face of each who passed in. He had had too much vodka to do this to any great effect, and he let us through without demur, probably taking us for famished students, if he thought about us at all. Directly we got in we were confronted by a huge bar stocked with basins. A boy was serving out cabbage soup at a farthing a basinful. Another boy was serving out *kasha,* also at a farthing a basin. On a green notice-board, among an array of vodka bottles, I read the following queer price-list:

Lodging	3 farthings
black bread	,,
soup	1 farthing
kasha	1 ,,
fish	2 farthings
tea	1 farthing
beer	3 farthings
shirt (dirty)	3 ,,
A pair of old trousers . . .	30 ,,
coat	30 ,,
A pair of old boots . . .	10 ,,

The doss-house was owned by a merchant who made a handsome profit out of it, I am told. So well he might! The accommodation was *nil*. Straw to sleep upon. No chairs beyond three park seats. Two rooms lit by two jets of gas each. A small lavatory that might even make a beggar faint. Men and women slept in the same room, though they were, for the most part, so degraded that it scarcely occurred to one that they were of different sex.

We went upstairs; the air seemed a trifle less odorous there. Even there we agreed it was impossible to stay. About a hundred beggars were already asleep, and most of the rest were making themselves comfortable.

It was a large dark room, unventilated, and having all the windows sealed with putty, so that not the slightest draught of air came through. There were, of course, no fires in the room; it was heated by hot-water pipes. One would say the floor had not been cleaned since the day it was first used. It was rotten and broken and covered with black slime. The snow from the beggars' boots melted in the warm room, as it had done every night this winter. Huge gnawn holes in the cornice showed where the rats had been. Yet in this den, on such a floor, human beings lay and slept! Pigs would have been housed better.

Yet in a gloomy corner opposite the entrance a little lamp burned before the sacred picture of Jesus. The Ikon stood there and looked uopn the scene. It seemed to say, "God is here also, He does not disclaim even this; and in His sight even these are men and have souls."

A Socialist government would make a difference in a place like this. The walls would be of white tiles and would shine like a station on the electric railway. There would be couches and mattresses, parqueted floors, electric light, baths, a reading-room next door, a free restaurant below. And there would be no Ikon. They would feel they didn't need the sanction of God for what the reason approved.

I said this to Nicholas. He had bought a bottle of vodka, and was treating a man who said he was an ex-student and literary man.

"Shouldn't we enjoy ourselves!" said the man.

"Nice mess they'd make of it," said Nicholas.

"They'd have to clean the beggars and dress them, and then shut up the pawnshops and the vodka shops, and then give them some work."

"None of the beggars will do any work in the winter," said the man; "there are workhouses already, but they won't go there. There's more fun on the streets, and then our work is more acceptable to God; we keep the people charitable. We stand outside taverns and theatres and tobacconists, and by our poverty remind the customers of God's blessings. We restrain their self-indulgence."

This was evidently an impossible line of argument. I asked him how the people came to be beggars. In his case it was vodka, and he had met scores of students reduced to the same plight. Most of the beggars were just tramp labourers, in the summer they would go to the country again; the women were the off-scourings of the streets. There were many more women beggars than men, but they died off more quickly. "The *intelligentia* of Moscow lead such a life," said he. "The very Socialists, who want to make the place clean, lead dirty lives themselves. Look at the hundreds of girls shouting themselves deaf on the Tverskoe Boulevard, look at the students arm-in-arm with them, think of the average middle-class Russian's life. He gorges himself with food, rots his mind with French novels, and openly confesses what women are to him."

" We shall have to get rid of the reformers before we shall reform Russia," said Nicholas, solemnly.

" Oh, I don't blame them," said the beggar; " it's all part of life; we beggars are all manure, that's what we are; they plaster us about the roots of Society and make the little red blossoms grow—and the white blossoms."

" It's all very dirty," I remarked.

" One learns to understand dirt, to love it even. God made the dirt; see how the picture looks down, the eyes don't blink." He pointed to the Ikon.

" Dirt is part of the Russian harmony," I suggested with a smile.

" Yes," said the beggar, " perhaps one day it will all be different, and we shall have a vote and pay taxes and have jobs as well as wives and families. But, you know, ' you must love us whilst we are dirty, for everyone will love us when we are clean.' "

A STREET SHRINE, MOSCOW

PASSION MONASTERY, MOSCOW

CHAPTER VII

A NIGHT AT A SHRINE

LIFE at Moscow was very full during the ensuing two months. What the students did I did. Each night there was some new diversion; a visit to the Narodny Dom with dancing and confetti fights until three in the morning, or a skating masquerade at Chisty Prudy. Sometimes we would go in sledges to Petrovsky Park; other times we would go to the Kremlin and climb up the steeple of St John's. These days were full of variety and entertainment. One evening I presented myself at the stage-door of the Theatre of Art; I could not find the box-office. Stanislavsky's company was performing *The Life of Man.* An actor met me and I asked him how I should get a ticket. But, when he discovered I was an Englishman, he took me to the manager, and got me a free pass to the third row of the stalls. That was glorious hospitality. It was a magnificent performance; the stage management was perfect if extremely ingenious. Another night a Russian girl asked me to take her to the Hermitage Theatre; she was going anyway, but she needed a " cavalier."

So we went and listened to four French farces, all performed the same night. Katia, for so she was called, was a Georgian and talked to me of the Caucasus all the time we promenaded. In Russian theatres one has a quarter of an hour's promenade after each act. We were supposed to be immensely smitten with one another, and ignorant of the state of my heart she said sweetly, as we were in the sledge going home, "You were a quiet boy and I awakened you, eh?"

Among a number of expeditions, visiting factory owners, tobogganing at Sokolniky, or skiing, one adventure stands out more vividly than the others. Phrosia, a lame woman who cooked for us in our Kislovka room, had warned us she wouldn't be at home for two days. She was going away to pray. Shura wanted to know why she couldn't remain in Moscow to pray, but she only looked at him very solemnly and said her mother had always prayed at Troitsky Lavra that day and so would she. I resolved to accompany her. The account of my pilgrimage which I wrote at the time will show the sequel.

"SERGIEVO, 2.30 a.m.

"This is written in the waiting-room here. Before me the lights twinkle on the little vodka bar. There is much noise in the room, but the heavy sound of snoring is gaining the victory over all. What a night this has been! How came I here? How is it that I still live? To-night—the first act was among crowds of pilgrims at church; the second act in a one-room cottage framed in old newspapers and inhabited by five men, two women and two babies (thoughts of plague and exit!); the third act was spent among the churches and the stars in the cool, fresh night; fourth act, discovery of the railway station full of people drunk or sleeping; the fifth act is to come. I am drinking my eleventh glass of tea from the inexhaustible pot, but ah! how restless I am! I am sure I carry on my person many of the unnumbered inhabitants of that cottage. How the insects creaked in its newspaper walls! About me now, picture fearful, monstrous peasants spluttering, roaring, singing. A gentleman comes along now and then and pretends to keep order. My *vis-à-vis* is uproarious. Figure him with thick red hair and wild red beard. He is a fat man and he stands facing the *gendarme* and answers each remonstrance with an inarticulate roar. Rrrr! His hair has been cut away with shears, and it overhangs his head equally all round like the straw of a thatched cottage.

" 'Make w-way, will you,' said the peasant to me with a voice like thunder.

" I smiled gently. The peasant frowned and twisted his red lips under his tangled moustache. He leaned down and brought his wild phiz close up to mine and leered into my eyes. I could not have dreamed of a more terrifying face. It recalled to me the dreadful thoughts of my childhood as to what might be the face of the Black Douglas or the Bogey Man.

" 'Make way, will you, or I'll cut your throat,' he roared.

" Several of his companions warned him that the *gendarme* was listening.

" 'You're not very polite,' I said. 'What is it you want?'

" 'There's no room for me anywhere else.'

" I made a place for him and he took it without a word. He became immediately content and self-absorbed like a babe that, after crying and kicking, has found its mother's breast.

" He is now sitting with both elbows on the table. In one hand he grasps a fish tightly; he held that fish in his hand all the time he was confronting me. Ah! Now he is yelling to the counter for vodka. He is a rough customer. A tall labourer in a red shirt bent over to me just now and asked me if I knew what his name was.

" 'His name is Dung.'

" Everyone in the room laughed. Even the *gendarme* grinned. The peasant repeated his joke. It was evidently his only stock and store. Perhaps his father taught him that joke, and he in his turn had it from his grandfather. He is at this moment addressing the peasant of the human thatch.

"'Mr Dung, ha, ha, ha. Your Excellency Baron Dung, a word with you, ha, ha, ha,' etc. etc. etc. But, strange to say, my antagonist pays no attention whatever, but regards his fish and his, as yet, untasted, vodka with the eye of an expert mathematician who is pondering some more-than-usually-interesting problem.

"There has not been much occasion for *ennui* since I came in here. A Lettish pedlar has come in, he has a face like an American music-hall hobo, a tramp artiste. So you would say to see his high-arched eyebrows and his long mouth. But he is a poor starved wretch, and there may be some truth in his reiterated assertion that he has been robbed of three farthings. If he doesn't stop screeching out that fact the *gendarme* is likely to throw him out or take him to the 'lock-up.' My attention is divided between him and a girl at the bar. During the last ten minutes a peasant lass has taken five glasses of vodka, and a well-dressed man, himself drunk, is making clumsy attempts to kiss her. She grins and reels about—a country girl. She smiles idiotically and tries to steer her cheek and lips away from the man's moustache. If he were a little less unsteady on his feet he would have no difficulty, I am sure. The man is making us all a speech now, and the peasants are jesting according to their knowledge of jests. The *gendarme* strolls fretfully up and down, his fingers twitching. Oh, my acquaintance with the one joke has risen and is addressing the man who has been 'treating' the girl. He caught hold of the man with the thatched head; the latter rose, thinking the policeman wanted him. But no!

"'Allow me to introduce you to Mr—'

"'Here, I've heard enough of that, you go out,' says the *gendarme*, and grasps the joking man to put him out.

"Then up speaks the pedlar.

"'Please, Mr Gendarme, he stole three farthings of mine.'

"'Yes?' replies the policeman. 'Then you must both come to the police-station.' He blows his whistle vigorously. There is a crowd of moujiks round him. The man with the thatched head has sunk back sleepily into his seat. I hear him murmuring gently, 'Cut his throat, cut his throat.' Two other *gendarmes* are here now, and the two prisoners are being kicked out with great turbulence.

"A furious noise, and yet many men and women are lying fast asleep among the bundles on the floor. The bar-tender moves hither and thither behind his orderly rows of glass bottles and is quite at his ease. He is bringing me an extra pennyworth of sugar now! In the darkest corner of the waiting-room an elaborate temple is set up and little lamps burn dimly before the gilded Ikons of Mary and the child Jesus. The drunkards look thither furtively and cross themselves. The scene is strange. I was rummaging through my pocket-book just now for some paper and came across the photograph of dear K——. I took it out and let the face look into the room. I felt convulsed with laughter at the wistful way she looked out upon the scene; the print is fading slightly, and there is a sort of 'silken, sad, uncertain' expression about it that was so astonishingly true that the real face could not look differently if my friend could be instantly brought here. But she sleeps peacefully in that London suburb that I know. Fourteen hours to wait for a train! And what shall I do this long day? I might walk back again to Moscow, thirty-five versts is not far, but it has come to my mind that I shall not walk this stretch. It has been a rough jaunt.

"This room with its vodka bar and its temple of God, and the drunkards flung all around the steps of the altar, is a picture of Russia—of an aspect of Russia. When I came into the village this afternoon the sacred Ikons were being borne in procession through the streets, and services were being conducted at street corners. Two priests were detailed off to officiate at this station. I saw them go in through the throng of the bare-headed crowd. Dressed in cloth of gold and mitred in purple, they moved about majestically in the performance of their office, and from their mouths came the unearthly sounds in which it is orthodox to clothe the words of their litany. Pilgrimages are made to this shrine on each great fast day. Many thousands flock hither from Moscow and from the country round about; some come on foot, some by train, and some in sledges. I came by train, third-class, with our cook; she is now somewhere sleeping in an unheavenly cottage there below. It has been interesting to see the far-distance pilgrims; the peasant women bent double by huge bundles on their backs, but resting on stout staffs and looking out very piously and anciently from their deep hoods. We had four of them in our carriage in the train; very gay they looked in their coloured cotton dresses; but they were reserved, and their monosyllabic groans and grunts scarcely sounded articulate outside the circle of their own company. The service last evening was grand; the festival commenced at six o'clock; I had been watching the crows whirling about the domes of the churches, settling on the high gilt crosses, flapping their wings, balancing themselves, calling to one another, and the dusk was deepening. I went into the great church and looked at the long queue of people waiting to consecrate their candles and be anointed with the holy oil. At last the priests came forward and lit one candle before each of the Ikons, and a long-haired pope stood before the people and pronounced the induction of the service. The choir voices swelled in unison as the incense reached one's senses, and the solemn litany went forward with its eternal choric response: 'Oh, Lord, have mercy, oh, Lord, have mercy.' '*Gospody pomeely, Gospody pomeely.*' . . . And now and then the priest would repeat the words so rapidly that it sounded like gospodipity, gospodipity.

" About ten o'clock I left the dim church and went out into the darkness, among shadows of unknown men and women and bundles. A hundred yards distant a bright window gave a full light on to the night. A tavern was there, ' where stood a company with heated eyes,' a wild, hairy people who stormed and screamed and fell about. A glass of tea for me, also a bottle of black-currant water; the like of the latter we shall not drink again. No room to sit there. The street without was full of solicitous boys and girls who wanted to find you a lodging. To one of these I had recourse, and after many unsuccessful ventures she took me to the forementioned cottage. There was more adventure and novelty than sleep on the bill of fare, and I was tempted. When one carries a portable bed one is fairly independent, but why had I no misgivings here? The great winter stove on which the good woman of the place bakes her bread had been at full heat all day, and the men and women who lay there were like lumps of flesh in a thick stew of air. On the torn newspaper ceiling the flies walked about or buzzed down to settle on the faces of the sleepers. The place of honour was given me, the one bed with a rag of curtain. I was blessed and prayed for before the cottage Ikons, which were set up in a further corner — perhaps I had need for prayer. . .

"At midnight, having passed through many adventures, I evacuated the position. Much difficulty there was among the legs of the sleepers, but an exit was achieved, and presently there was a ceiling of stars above me and a cold breeze about. The cottage being in the middle of a field there was some further difficulty in extrication. Then came a series of *rencontres*. First a beggar, very drunk, and whirling a cudgel above his head, tells me he knows me, has seen me in Moscow. (I wondered if, perhaps, he had actually seen me at the night-house with Nicholas.) Then a *gendarme* presents a bold aspect but falls back judiciously since I do not hesitate in my stride. I am a suspicious-looking character. Watchmen-monks, with the night breeze blowing their long hair about (the clergy all wear long hair), I have encounters with these. But the night was very good and full of music; never so many stars, never such a Milky Way or such black unstarry patches, and the air was thrilling. The newspaper cottage was far away. Presently I discovered the railway station and the waiting-room full of people, and here I am. It will soon be dawn. I have poured myself out the twelfth and thirteenth glasses of tea, very like hot water and without sugar or milk. If I have caught any malady at the cottage I should be saved by this internal washing. I become the latest convert to the system of

Dr Sangrado of *Gil Blas* memory. . . . Two priests have arrived in the waiting-room. . . .

" Ah! I hear that, after all, there will be a train home soon.

" I left the station at a run and was back at the newspaper cottage, and a half-dressed, half-sleeping woman let me in, got me my things and asked mournfully why it was I could not sleep.

" ' Was it too hot, barin? '

" She blessed me and let me depart.

" Now the little village was in movement, the church bell was sounding and many little bells were tinkling; and many sleepy folks were making their way to church, for at dawn another great service commenced. At the waiting-room a service was begun. And now the night gave way to early dusk, and the dark churches became dimly visible; the sleepy peasants rubbed their eyes. Presently a glorious sunrise began to flush upon the gold and silver Ikons, and softly and lowly with the incoming light the services in the churches proceeded, in sweet, melancholy music. The faces of the worshippers became less shadowy, and at last all was in full day. Then, too, my lazy train steamed away, and Sergievo and last night were both behind me."

CHAPTER VIII

THE DAY AFTER THE FEAST

THE day after a church festival is always the Feast of St Lombard. Outside all the pawnbrokers' establishments one sees crowds of poor people drawn up in line—men, women, children, but mostly women. It is a pitiable sight. Each person is carrying the article to be pledged, and whether it be a samovar or a chair, or a petticoat or a pair of trousers, it is never wrapped up. Russians are not ashamed. The queue which I saw near the Tverskaya a street long, the day after my return from Sergievo, would have been thought a disgrace to any English city, but the Russians looked on with equanimity. And to walk from end to end, from the pawnbroker's door to the last person who has just hurried up with a pledge, was like reading a chapter from the darkest pages of Gorky. One sees children of sad aspect, with bewildered eyes; young girls as yet honest and clean, but selling the last things of a home; raging women, weeping women and laughing women, drunkards and drudges; or besotted men of the sort who drink away their wives' and daughters' honour, hopeless home thieves who would steal away even the clothes from a bed and turn them into vodka. It is notable that in Russia, as yet, it is chiefly the men who drink; a drunken woman is very rare. The woman in Russia is the wisest and strongest person in the home. One poor woman, stout and rubicund, but of countenance preternaturally solemn, seemed to me weighed down with responsibility. She had a copper samovar under her arm, and I asked her what misfortune had overtaken her. It was the old story; her husband was a cabman, he ought to have taken no holiday yesterday, the streets were full of people and he might have had many fares, but he went to a tavern in the morning, and spent all his money and fought with a man and was arrested by a *gendarme*. I asked her how much she would get " on " the samovar. " Seventy-five copecks, barin," she replied. " Have you got another samovar?" I asked. " No, barin, we shall have to borrow water; I don't know what the table will look like without the samovar, it won't be home without it, it has always been on the table; it was my mother's, and she gave it me when I was married. I am sure we shall never have good fortune after the samovar has gone."

I lent her seventy-five copecks—one shilling and sixpence—and told her to take her beloved samovar home again. She accepted without hesitation. She put the samovar down on the pavement and embraced me with both arms. " Bless you, barin, the Lord bless you; come along and have some tea."

I went to her poor little home—two rooms—in which there was no furniture beyond the bed, a table, some boxes and the Ikons. Two pallid, starved daughters, girls of thirteen and sixteen, smiled sweetly and made themselves happy over our party. I had bought some *barankas,* dry Russian biscuits, *en route.*

The woman told me the story of how her husband had nearly been cured of drunkenness by God. A year or two ago a most holy priest at Sergievo had been empowered by God to cure drunkenness. Thousands and thousands, tens of thousands of drunkards had made pilgrimages from Moscow and Kiev and Odessa and the country, and had been cured by the priest by miracle, and Vania had gone from Moscow and had been a whole month sober, because of the prayer of the holy man. Then suddenly the holy man was removed and Vania got drunk again.

It was like this. Vania went on foot to Sergievo and saw the monk. First he was anointed, and then received communion, and then he went to the priest's house, where he had to tell his story to the holy man. Then they prayed before the Ikon that God would have mercy upon Vania. After the prayer the priest rose and said, " God knows now that you want to become sober and lead a new life. You must remember that

He is looking at you particularly, just as He would at a new plant that was beginning to bud. To-day He sees you all white and beautiful, and He says to the angels, 'Look at my servant Vania, how well he is living.' Each morning and evening God will say how much brighter and more beautiful he is becoming."

" *Slav Bogou,* Glory be to God," replied Vania.

" Now," said the priest, " for how many days can you keep sober, for how many days can you live without touching a drop of beer or vodka? "

" For ever, a thousand days," replied Vania.

" A thousand days is only three years; it's not for ever," said the priest.

Vania blinked his eyes.

" You must kneel on your knees and swear to God that you will not drink," said the priest. " But if you break the vow it will be very dreadful."

" Yes," said Vania, " I shall swear it."

" You are very weak," said the priest; " you must pray God each morning when you get up and each night before you go to bed that He may give you strength. Perhaps you will fail, perhaps you are lost, but God is going to give you a chance. He's going to watch you for one week first, for one little week. You must swear to God that you will not drink vodka or beer for one week."

Vania, on his knees, repeated the oath after the priest.

" Rise now, Vania," said the priest; " I think you will keep this little oath, but if you feel you can't you must come straight to me and I will release you. You mustn't break it. I can let you off quite easily if you come to me. But if you break it, God may strike you dead, or He may give you to the Devil. The Devil would be very glad to have you, Vania, but it would be very bad for you. To-day is Sunday; I shan't be angry if you come to me to-morrow or on Tuesday and say, ' Release me, father.' I will then release you and pray God to have mercy on you and to send angels to help you."

Vania went away and kept his vow on Monday, Tuesday, Wednesday, Thursday, but on Friday, a very cold day, he wanted a drink very badly. Comrades laughed at him, too. He drove up and down the city and got only one little fare the whole morning. There were fifteen copecks in his pocket. He might get two glasses for that. Every tavern tempted, and the Devil seemed waiting at every tavern-door. At two o'clock he drove home quickly and gave the fifteen copecks to his wife; at half-past two he rushed home again and begged the fifteen copecks back. He entered the shop and placed his bottle on the counter and asked for vodka. The woman behind the railing of the " monopoly " counter stepped back to pick out what he wanted, and at that moment Vania, all of a tremble, looked up and saw the holy Ikon in the shop, a figure of Christ staring at him. The woman, when she brought the bottle, thought the customer had a fit, for he suddenly shrieked and bolted from the shop.

" Oh, Lord, have mercy! "

On Friday night Vania saw the priest again and asked to be released. The priest praised him and prayed with him and offered him release, and then Vania would not take it. He asked to swear again. So he was sworn in again and this time for ten days.

Vania went home and prayed, and successfully resisted temptation for ten days, and very proud he was at the end of that time when he returned to the holy man and the latter praised him and hung a sign of God by a little chain round his neck.

The priest prayed with him again and sent him away for a fortnight on the same conditions.

Vania was sober in this way for a whole month, and all his family with him, and he prospered with his cab and bought their furniture out of pawn. God was evidently very pleased with Vania.

But at the end of that time a catastrophe happened. Vania went to the shrine to be re-confirmed in his new life, and behold the priest was not there any more. He had been removed by the Bishop, and no one knew where he had gone to. There was unutterable sadness and despair in the crowds of drunkards that Vania found there, weeping and gnashing of teeth.

The Government, hearing of the success of the priest, and noting the diminution in the sale of vodka, had suppressed the holy man in order that there might be no shortage in the treasury. There was the interest on foreign loans to pay!

CHAPTER IX

A MUSHROOM FAIR IN LENT

I HAD been out one morning looking at St Saviour's and tasting the March sunshine, and I returned to the Kislovka unexpectedly. Nicholas, taken by surprise, was grinding at mathematics very gloomily. I had never seen him so despondent, so melancholy. He looked at me very sadly when I sat down beside him and began to chat.

" Why are you going to leave me? " he asked. I had told him that I should not remain in Moscow beyond Easter, and we were then in Lent. " Why will you not wait till June and then we can go to Lisitchansk together; and we will walk to the Caucasus, or we will walk across Europe to Calais and get back to England? "

Poor boy! There was no answer that would please him. Moscow had no attraction for me once the snow was off the ground and the country lay open, tempting me. Moscow was too comfortable a place; but that I had not English friends it was as comfortable as London, and I was—" full of malice against the seductions of dependency."

Whilst I was sitting talking to Nicholas I noticed

that the mirror in the room had been covered over with newspapers, and I wondered why.

" Why is the mirror covered up? " I asked.

Nicholas looked at it absent-mindedly, and then blushed.

" Oh, I was walking up and down and didn't want to see myself," he replied. " Every time I got up to that wall I saw my silly face till I got quite angry and covered it up."

I comforted him.

He cheered up, but when I said I was going out again he put on his things to come with me, and implored me not to leave him all day or he might commit suicide. " What shall we do then? " I asked. " Let's go down to the Mushroom Fair on the quayside; but first we'll have some lunch."

The pious Russian eats no meat in Lent. Once the Carnival, with its burst of drinking and feasting, is over, the Day of Forgiveness past (a sort of Old Year's Night festival), and Ash Wednesday has signalised itself by a day-long tolling of bells for prayers, the true Slav enters upon a time of rigorous self-denial. Nominally he lives wholly upon Lenten oil; in actual practice he generally manages to find something more sustaining —different sorts of porridge, fruit jellies, mushroom soups and the like. Nicholas and I went into a students' eating-house, and neither of us were in the least orthodox in the matter of food. I judged that my companion would be benefited by a large plate of roast beef and gherkins and baked potatoes, and this we accordingly sat down to.

Vegetables are expensive in Moscow at this season of the year—an ordinary vegetarian restaurant dinner costs three or four shillings—and there is, therefore, a first-rate market for any of the past summer or autumn's produce that the peasant can bring in. About mid-March the Moscow peasants' Mushroom Fair takes place, and there is a grand turnover of greasy roubles and copecks at that busy market. The country peasant has awakened from his winter sleep to go on his first adventure and work of the year, for as yet his fields are deep in snow and Jack Frost will not be vanquished for another month. The mushrooms that, with the help of his wife and children, he gathered in the autumn are all frozen together in the casks at the back of his izba; the planks and boards of his sledge, van and market stall lie frozen together among the drifts and icicles. A rough jaunt this year! March came in with great winds and snowstorms. The track of the road is an even wilderness of snow. Yet for the fifty or even one hundred miles that the peasant comes to this honey fair he finds his road, and battles gaily forward. Through drift, over stream, skirting the great forest, he goes on with many a slip and tumble, the dry snow blowing up and down in a Russian snow mist. Wrapped up in sacking and sheepskin, he sits among his casks and trestles, sings or sleeps or talks to his horse, every now and then standing up and pulling the horse round by his rope reins with a " Gently, Vaska," or " Curse you, Herod."

During the first week in Lent he arrives at Moscow, and every year at that time one may see the long line of stalls and booths newly rigged up on the quayside of the river, below the Kremlin walls. This year it has snowed heavily every day, and the wind had blown the stalls about and drifted the snow over the merchandise. It was snowing when Nicholas and I arrived, and the large flakes were settling on the honey and the oil and the mushrooms, and dissolving as we watched them. We kicked our way through the deep snow on the uneven ground, with a merry crowd laughing and chaffering. The Moscow old-wife was very busy. She is a fat, rank, jolly woman, more like the old-wives of Berwick than those of any other place in Europe, perhaps. Figure the old gossips buying, gingerly sampling and tasting, dipping in a huge vat of soaking mushrooms and taking a Rabelaisian mouthful from a great wooden spoon, or holding a dripping yellow-green mushroom between a fat thumb and fore-finger. There were also women in charge of some of the stalls—peasant wives, fat, laughing, healthy women. The wind blew fresh against the rosy cheeks of a gay crowd, for the market was truly half a revel and a game. It was a fair, but quite a strange one. What an array of clumsy casks, all these full of very mushy-looking mushrooms soaking in oil or vinegar. Then there were ropes of dried mushrooms, tied as we tie daisy-chains in England. But it is not only a Mushroom Fair. At the corner by the bridge there was a huge pile of bright red berries; the peasant in charge insisted on calling me Prince. The scene remains quite vivid in my memory. These were cranberries; they can be stewed into a fine-looking pudding. *Kisel:* sour jelly, they call it; it is bright crimson and looks too good to eat. Boys were running about with stuffed birds—crows, magpies, jays—that the country youths stuffed in the autumn. One could buy all sorts of things, even inlaid chess-tables and hand-made chess-men. At one side a youth was selling calico that had been in a fire; there was a crowd about him and a Petticoat-Lane-like-bidding going on. Next to him was a place for buying plaster saints and holy pictures. The next stall was occupied by a man with hot pies—piping hot yellow puffs full of mushroom and cauliflower—and, *vis-à-vis*, a huge steaming samovar from which a thirsty throng were getting tea at 1d. a glass. Perhaps the most Russian sight was the huge piles of clumsy wooden implements hacked out of pine with the all-useful adze. A sea of Russian basins, of chests, trays, and all kinds of boxes. Then there was the pottery department, a fine place for buying queer pots. If you wished to buy mushrooms in oil you had first to go and buy a pot; you obtained a strange brown vase, looking like a Roman urn. You wanted to buy jam—you must first buy a pot. A stall over the way is heaped up with honey—hard, frozen honey. We were invited to buy. " Only fivepence a pound," said the man. We bought half a pound and received it in a piece of newspaper, a sheet of the *Novoe Vremya*. Most of the customers of the fair bought green rush baskets for a few pence, and in these put dried mushrooms, dried fruits for compôte, cranberries and the like. The vendor of the honey had driven in from Toula, a town in the vicinity of Tolstoy's estate. I thought I might get some first-hand information about the great novelist, so I asked:

" How is Tolstoy? "

" I don't know. Who is he? Is he a wrestler? " he replied.

Evidently the prophet was not unknown but in his own country.

This fair is a great chance to see the Russian peasant with his own produce. Visitors to Moscow in Lent are seldom shown this really interesting sight, much more humanly interesting than the Kremlin, the churches and museums. For Russia can boast of very little antiquity in her civilisation or her buildings. Much more interesting than her little past is her present.

At the fair all is Russian—even the oranges and lemons come from the groves of South Russia and the Caucasus. One gets another glimpse of the Russian harmony, the harmony of which the winter, the forests, the church, the peasants, the beggars are integral parts. This Russian life is actually organic, and all that is of it is necessarily akin to all. This picture is undiscordant. Happy, rude, contented Russia! All these old-world folk are like grown-up children playing shop with mud-pies. What careless laughter rings about this snowy fair; what absurd wit and earthly humour! Crowds of jokes are about—mostly of the low Chaucerian kind. Indeed, one cannot help asking how much this fair has changed since the fourteenth century. Nature has turned out mushrooms, cranberries, crab-apples, oranges, honey, Russian men and women in just about the same cast as she does to-day—and probably even the hand-made chess-men differed little from these on sale now. The world does not change very much.

CHAPTER X

DEPARTURE FROM MOSCOW

ALL the winter I had been in correspondence with Kharkov in connection with my lost luggage. Early in April I received a notification that the box had been found. The Customs House then sent me in a bill of charges, so much for every day the box had remained in their possession. The railway and Customs made two pounds profit out of the loss of my box; they actually charged me for the loss! So slowly, moreover, did the business go forward that it seemed to me I should not recover my property before I left Moscow. Even after they received the money they seemed in no hurry to proceed. But one day I did actually go out to a goods station and get my box into a sledge and take it home. The end was sudden, so sudden that I could not help laughing at the contrast. A carter took me down into a dark cellar to identify the box, and the said box, high up among large packing-cases, was identified. In its transit from that high position to *terra firma* it managed to displace a quarter of a ton case, which came down with a crash like thunder. We were both knocked down, and both very badly bruised, though I think the carter came off second best; a stream of blood was pouring down his face. " Oh, Lord God! " I heard him exclaim. He was looking at the Ikon in the room; it sounded as if he was swearing at it.

" Any limbs broken? " said he.

" No."

" Then, praise the Lord! There's your box."

Two days after this there was an immense thaw and the sledges gave way to wheeled carriages. On the Wednesday it had been a white city; on Thursday it was black and there was not a sledge to be seen. The sun had been getting hotter and winning its way each day, just a little, against the snow, and then suddenly one night a west wind swept in from Europe and the Atlantic, and with it a flood of rain. Winter was drowned. No one was sorry; for winter by all accounts had stayed too long. The Sunday was Palm Sunday, the day of branches. The Russians call it *Verba*, and it is a great festival in Moscow. Shura and Nicholas and I went to the Kremlin to enjoy the sights.

It was a day of ecstasy. The sun shone as it had not done since I came to Moscow. It was suddenly full of promise, and one felt the promise in one's blood. One's fingers tingled with the desire to live, the eyes rested with envy upon the green branches that the people carried. In the Kremlin there was a din as of a carnival. Ten thousand silly squeakers and hooters sounded in the air. Inflated pigs were expiring, ridiculous sausages were deflating and collapsing, toy geese were quacking, boys and girls were blowing whistles and trumpets, and students also were blowing, and even staid old gentlemen. This day commemorated the triumphal entry into Jerusalem; it was also the triumphal entry of spring into Moscow, of life into death. The crowd huzzaing was delirious with the news that the winter was over. Even the rich people in their carriages, passing in solemn state into the Kremlin, seemed part of the new life. They were all in spring dresses—the women in purples and soft greens, and the men in light tweeds.

It seemed to me, however, that those on foot were having the gayer time. We were crushed as tightly as I have ever been in a London crowd. Everyone was laughing and chaffing, especially the girl students from the University, and the confetti was flying thick and fast.

Verba week was my last in Moscow. On Easter Sunday I left for the South.

Easter Eve came at last, the greatest night in the Russian holy year. At midnight we were all in the Kremlin, that is, I was there, and Nicholas and Shura, and everyone else in Moscow surely. Phrosia, the servant whom I had accompanied to the shrine at Sergievo, had taken a large sweet Easter loaf and a cake of sugar-cream, *paskha*, to be consecrated at church.

I saw her in a yard outside the little monastery in the Petrovka. There were two or three hundred cakes waiting with hers, all set out on informal tables on trestles. In the centre of each cake a wax candle was burning. Each table was a little forest of candles, some long, some short, some just lit, and some burning out. Every now and then a priest came and took a cake into the church just as the candle was expiring. Phrosia had evidently just come, for the candle on her *pashka* was newly lit. The church was a casket, a precious case of gems. The priests moving to and fro, the pale faces of the Ikons lit up by many candles seemed the glamour of a fairy tale. The cakes being brought in, the priest sprinkling holy water, seemed rites which I, a mortal, only saw by accident. Indeed, any Englishman would have found Easter Night strange and wonderful. It is one of the two occasions in the year when one can see again what is below the surface of Moscow life of to-day. One can see what Moscow was before it became so commercialised. At six o'clock on Easter Eve the electric trams cease to run; from that moment Moscow becomes the holy city of old time. The strange mystery and sacredness which must have enwrapped it in ancient days is again felt in the streets. The shops are all shut and dark, the churches are all open and bright. The thousand-and-one street temples are decorated with coloured lamps, the doors stand wide open, the sacred faces of the Ikons look out into the roads. Even the air is infected with church odours, and the multitudinous domes of purple and gold rest above the houses in enigmatical solemnity—they might be tents and pavilions of spirits from another world.

In the streets men and women are carrying lighted candles hither and thither, and every now and then one sees a person carrying his *paskha* cake to church. Outside the Cathedral of the Annunciation a regiment of guards is drawn up and an officer is giving them instructions as to the duties for the night. Presently the rich and aristocratic families of Moscow will drive up one by one to do homage to the Ikons in the cathedral. At midnight the Kremlin is so thronged that it is difficult to move. All are waiting for the *Resurrection*, all are waiting for the booming forth of the great bell of St John's Church, the largest bell of Moscow and of Russia, rung only once a year. That will signify that "Christ has risen." The priests are praying before the Ikons and searching their hearts. Shortly after midnight they will rise from their knees and announce to the people, "We have found him. He is risen. *Christos Voskrece.*"

I wandered among the merry crowds to the tower of St John's, and as I was passing the great cannon, the Tsar of cannons, I overheard someone speaking English. I directed my steps in that direction and found the people, two clean-shaven young men, in English clothes, high English collars and bowler hats—immaculately English. They were talking loudly, evidently taking it for granted that no one could understand them. I took up my stand quite close and listened. This is what I overheard. It was very small talk, but it sounded very strange to hear it in this Russian crowd.

"The Moscow people are very rough, they've no manners at all. They don't care who they jostle or push as long as they get along."

"Yes, I was going through one of the Kremlin gates yesterday and a fellow knocked my hat off. Of course it was very nice of him, but he didn't stop to tell me why he did it. I thought he was mad, but they told me afterwards it was a sacred gate. I saw several people take off their hats as they went through. They say the sentry has orders to fire on anyone who does not lift his hat. I felt I wanted to apologise to someone. It's a beautiful custom, and I hadn't any intention of infringing the law. I believe in doing as Rome does in Rome. I wonder if the sentry would shoot. Nice row there'd be if they shot a British subject."

"You're right, but what'd they care. They're a rotten lot. I'd like to pole-axe the Governor. By-the-bye, have you heard anything of White recently? He said he thought his firm was sending him out."

"No."

"Did you know him at all? He was a thorough gentleman."

" No, not much; he didn't live my way, you know. I met him several times down the county ground."

" Yes, he was fairly mad over Surrey, wasn't he? We played many games together, he and I; he bowled an awfully tricky ball, a gentle lob-dob, nearly full pitch. You thought you were going to put it out of the ground for six, and then suddenly you found your wicket down."

At this point a disreputable beggar interrupted them.

" What d'you make of him—a drunken monk, eh? " said the cricketer. Both the Englishmen put on a look suggesting the principles of Political Economy, and signified by a frown that they did not encourage beggars. The " drunken monk," however, did not budge for five minutes, he looked up at them and grinned. The people all round grinned also and turned to watch the scene. Then, suddenly, the beggar, after churning his mouth for some time, spat on the Harris overcoat of the cricketer's companion and exclaimed:

" German pigs."

" Beast," said the Englishman, looking at his coat.

" They ought to be coming out soon. It's only a short procession, they say—out of the church round the wall and back again; then the bells will begin. It's after midnight now."

I moved away at this point and left the cricketer putting his watch to his ear to see if it was going. I had promised to meet Shura and Nicholas and go up into the steeple with them. I found them on one of the stone galleries where the little bells of the church nestle together. They had a collection of squibs and crackers and coloured lights which they were letting off so as to allow girl students below to pretend to be terrified.

"The priests have come out," said Nicholas, all at once pointing to a little procession just proceeding from the Uspensky. "*Christos Voskrece, Christos Voskrece,*" we heard all around us, and everyone was kissing one another. Then all the little bells of the churches began to tinkle, first a few and then more and more in confused ecstatic jangling Moscow bells do not sound in the least like English bells, the chime is not musical or solemn. Our bells chant, their bells cheer. On Easter Night it is ten thousand bells, the voice of a thousand churches praising God. A wild, astonishing clamour, and then suddenly came one sound greater in itself than all the little sounds put together, the appalling *boom* of the great bell of St John Veleeky:

"Ting a ling, ling, ling, ling,
Dong, dong, dong, dong, dong,
Ding, ding, dong a dong, ding,
Dang, dang, dang,
Ding, ding, ding, ding, ding, ding, ding,
DOOM . . *m* . *m m*!"

Suddenly Katia passed me—the girl I took to the theatre.

"*Christos Voskrece,*" said I, "Christ is risen."

"Yes," said she, "He is risen," and threw a handful of confetti in my eyes.

We all ate *paskha* cake together in the Kislovka room at three in the morning, and drank students' champagne, purchased by Shura at two shillings a bottle. So Easter Day dawned, my last at Moscow, the day of my parting with Nicholas, the day of my departure to the Caucasus.

CHAPTER XI

THE COMING OF SUMMER IN THE CAUCASUS

ANYTHING more wonderful than the change from winter to summer on the Caucasian mountain slopes could not easily be imagined. In April the plains were deep in snow, and in May, when English woods were leafing, every tree and bush looked stark and bare. Only by an occasional sallow in bloom one knew that the winter was over. The snowdrops and blue-bells sprang up in winter's traces, and then verdure danced out and clothed valley and slope up even to the summit of some low hills. The English spring, as I imagined it, was months ahead, but dawdled on among the cold winds; this hot summer overtook it at a bound and rushed on to its later glories, to the blossoming and fruiting of vine and pomegranate.

Of the wonderful things that happened in May it is difficult to write calmly. The fairies did not linger; they came trippingly, they waved their wands, they ran. The spells of green and gold were wrought, and charm moved over the land. The cowslip appeared, budded, blossomed, faded—in one short week. At quick step the dainty lilies of the valley came and took their place, and for three days glistened among grasses and ferns upon the rocks; and slender, graceful Solomon Seals stooped lovingly toward their sister lilies. Then hillsides suddenly blazed with yellow rhododendrons. Honeysuckle bloom came nestling in sunny corners among the rocks, then tall, sweet-scented bog-bean; ten varieties of orchis I found, and wild rose, wild strawberry and raspberry, wild vine, wild walnut, peach and pear and plum. In the grassy places, just dry after the last melted snow, out came the lizards, so that the plain literally squirmed with them, cunning, vicious little lizards basking in the sun, small and brown in May, but fat and green and speckled later, kissing at one another like snakes, and fond of biting off one another's tails. In the May sun the adder shot off from his damp sun-bath as one crushed through the scrub. The trees burst into leaf, first in the valleys and then on the hills. Each day one watched the climbing green and saw the fearful dark brow of a mountain soften away and pass from deep impenetrable black to soft laughing green. Snowy peaks lost their glory of white, and one knew them to be but little grey Grampians beside the huge mountains of Elbruz. The road-mud hardened and Persian stone-breakers were busy smashing their little heaps of boulders; in a week they had gone and the piles of rocks had become neat little heaps of flints. Then came terrific storms, a thunder-burst each week, and the rivers rose in their shingle beds and flooded off towards the Caspian and the Black Sea, carrying all manner of *débris* of uprooted shrub and tumbled rock. One soon saw the uses of the flints: they solidified the road. But, indeed, one day's sun sufficed to dry up a night's flood. The wild winds soon blew up the Sirocco—such dust storms that the whole landscape was for hours lost to the eyes. What of that—that was a day's unpleasantness to be covered by ample compensations. The sun was strengthening and its magic was awakening newer, richer colours than the English eye can care for, was working in strange new ways upon the soul mysteries and body mysteries of men and women. One knew oneself in the South, in the land of knives and songs. Every man seemed on horseback. The Georgian chiefs and the Ossetines and Cherkesses came careering along the military roads, their cartridge vests flashing, daggers gleaming. The *abreks* and *sheikhs* sprang down from the hills, appalling the lesser traffickers of the road, pilgrim, merchant, tramp, by their show of arms and bizarre effrontery. The strange hill shepherds, looking like antique Old-Testament characters, came marching before and behind their multitudinous flocks, with their four wolfish sheep-dogs in attendance and their camping waggons behind; from the mountain fastnesses they came, their faces one great flush of shining red, their eyes bathed in perspiration, blazing with light, their lank hair glistening. Often I lay beside the stream in the Dariel Gorge and watched flocks of a thousand or fifteen hundred sheep and goats pass by me. The lively mountain lambs, brown and black and white, very daring or short-sighted, would plunge three or four at a time into the stream beside me, would come up and stare in my face and bleat and then run away. Then the under-shepherds, who hold long poles and keep the marching order, would rush up and hurry them away from the water to the road, the procession of dust and woolly backs would slowly pass away to the music of the incessant calling of ewe and lamb.

The flocks are marched to the market towns, and big deals in hundreds and thousands of head of sheep are made. Or the shepherds encamp outside the town and send batches of sheep to be hawked through the streets. The Persian butchers come out and bid for their mutton. Boys run about the herd feeling the flesh of the sheep, masters weigh them in their arms or compare weights by holding a sheep in each hand. Each butcher takes one or two, or three or four, as he feels he is making a bargain or otherwise. One must not forget the twenty minutes' parley over prices. At last the business gets accomplished, and the flock goes on down the street to other butchers and leaves its little doomed contingent at each stall. On one occasion when I was watching, a lamb refused to be separated from a purchased brother, and, despite all efforts of the butcher and shepherd, came bleating back to the three

A GROUP OF CAUCASIAN SHEPHERDS

who were bought. The hillman hawker and the towns-man exchanged some witticism, and then the former struck a bargain and gave the affectionate lamb in cheap. I know the man's stall and once or twice have bought mutton there. The butcher does not slaughter all his sheep at once. First one goes and then another. One dead sheep or a part of one always hangs in his shop. All parts of the animal are sold at the same price, four-pence a pound, and customers do not, as a rule, specify leg or breast or neck, but simply the quantity they re-quire. When the butcher buys four sheep he kills one and hangs it in his shop, and the other three live ones are under the counter eating fodder or playing about among the customers' legs. The sheep-hawker makes his tour of the town and is all day at it, tramp, tramp, tramp, through mud or dust. In the evening one may see the muddied remnant of the flock, the rejected, the unsold, being driven wearily back to the main flock on the plains. Very melancholy the little party looks, and it is difficult to think them the fortunate ones, so woe-begone and wretched do they appear. All movement forward is a labour to them; not a few are lame, others have succumbed, and sometimes one sees the hawker with a dead lamb on his shoulder. No dogs are in attendance; none are needed.

There is plenty of money going in the town, plenty of wine and all good things for the up-country man when he cares to come in. With relief the house-heating is given up in April. Life becomes lighter, winter things are put away, windows are taken out, the summer wind begins to blow through all dwellings. The white-clad townsman takes his ice at his ease in the fresh air on the boulevards. The full, fat peasant eats as much as he can of pink and white and yellow for two copecks, and standing beside the ice-cream barrel, smacking his lips, testifies his appreciation by voluble remarks to passers-by. The Persian gunsmith sits in his open booth and inlays precious daggers, setting the handles with little constellations of stars. In glass cases, beside his shop, Caucasian belts and scimitars sparkle in the sun. There are streets of these workers where one might feel the sun was being robbed of his rays. One is in the land of the "Arabian Nights," from which nightmare and opium have been taken away. There is a gentleness, an ease and brightness not to be found in Little Russia or Moscow. Somewhat typical of this and wonderful in its way is the march of Russian regiments, the easy, swinging march, not quick, no, rather slow even, but pleasant and easy as for long distances. It was pleasant to regard a detachment of these marching so, their leaders singing a solo of a national hymn, the rest taking up the chorus. Pleasant also to listen to the singing of the workmen operating with the hand-crane at the riverside. There seemed to be general happiness and content among men as among animals. The sun bade love and life come from turf and rock and tree and man, and from man none the less than from the rest there came the answer unspoilt by self-sight and introspection. In scarlet and purple and blue came the answer. One saw all the truth as one looked at dark Georgian maidens trooping along a vineyard in May. To these this sun gave promise of a wine harvest.

CHAPTER XII

THE EPISTLE TO THE CAUCASIANS

MY kit for the Caucasus was composed of the following:—

A waterproof sleeping-sack,
A camel-hair blanket,
A pair of Georgian boots,
A flannel bashleek—a sort of hood to protect the head from cold,
Two suits of clothes—one of flannel, one of cloth,
A wadded overcoat,
A revolver,

and a trunk full of miscellaneous clothes. The books and papers of my recovered box I lent out to Moscow acquaintances or posted to England. My plan for the summer was to find an izba in the depths of the mountains and make a home there. On reaching Vladikavkaz Station I would put my luggage in the cloak-room and set out right away to tramp the mountains until I found what I wanted. Then I would return to Vladikavkaz and fetch my luggage in a cart.

Nicholas professed to be very much alarmed for my safety. He thought the place good, but he foresaw misadventures. He himself had been in Tiflis and Chiatouri in 1906 and had seen robbery and murder committed in broad daylight. He talked cut-throats for several days, and brought a number of students to back him up; he even urged that I take a trip down the Volga instead. But when he saw finally that I was not to be dissuaded, he promised to give me a letter of protection. He would write a letter to the Priests of the Caucasus. At each village I came to I should inquire where the *pope* lived and go to him at once and present my letter. I agreed: no doubt the priest in a village would know where there was an empty izba to be found, and he would help me to get it at a fair rate. So Nicholas wrote the following epistle:—

"*DEAR LITTLE FATHER,—Knowing that all our southern clergy are holily bound to give hospitality and help to fellowmen, I have taken upon myself the liberty—under unusual circumstances—to recommend to your care my friend, the Englishman Graham, who brings you this letter. I have taken, I repeat, the liberty upon myself to recommend him to your tenderness and care. He is an important man. I trust you will help him in his life in any way that stands within your power, that you will advise him in difficulty or introduce him to priests who can advise him. He may be often in danger among mountain people, and may have you only for a refuge. Money will not be necessary to him—only advice. As you are kind to him, may the Lord God be good to you and the holy work will be advanced, for Mr Graham is a writer who much loves Russia, is a great Christian, and writes many things about Russia and Russian things.—In confidence, I thank you,* *N—— L——.*"

Vladikavkaz is a town of forty thousand inhabitants, and is situated about two hundred miles from the Black Sea on the west, and from the Caspian on the east. It has been called the key of the Caucasus; it is certainly the most convenient town from which to enter. The English tourist, when he gets there, will be surprised to find it a European city with handsome buildings and shops, with a " Grand Hotel " and " Hotel Imperial " furnished as any other establishment of such name. There is a good service of electric trams and an abundance of two-horse cabs; very occasionally one may see a motor-car there. The people are, for the most part, Russians and Georgians, though there are great numbers of Ossetines, Tatars, Persians and Ingooshi. It is very interesting to watch the crowds of promenaders on the Alexandrovsky Boulevard on a festival; one sees men and women of almost every nationality under the Russian flag.

The Georgians, famous for their beauty, are the greatest dandies in the world. The young men, dressed in handsome and high-coloured tunics, well armed, show such extraordinarily slender and constricted waists that one is tempted to think they wear corsets. The leather belt round the middle of a young Georgian is strapped so tightly that he cannot use his legs freely. He walks in a jerky little swagger, swaying his shoulders ever so slightly from one side to another, and holding his head high. Then the Georgian and Ossetine girls are dark and arch; they are of large proportions and might not be thought attractive by English people. Their hair generally hangs down their backs in plaits, but is screened from view by coloured veils. They laugh and talk with ordinary freedom on the streets, and it never struck me that they lived very retired lives, as is reputed. In Vladikavkaz and in the Caucasus, however, the outsider sees little sign of love-making in the street. It is very exceptional to see a young couple, and as for kissing in public, I should say it must be the height of indelicacy—judging from the rarity of such a sight. I read in a modern English book that if a Georgian husband or wife were unfaithful, the offender and the co-respondent were exposed naked to the public gaze. If it is true it must afford an exciting spectacle. Apparently no divorce cases came on this summer.

The traveller can obtain very good lodging at Vladikavkaz, and French and German is spoken at the hotels. I stayed some days in a hotel which I found most comfortable. The nights as yet were probably cold for sleeping out, and I doubted the possibility of getting safely housed in mountain villages. For some time I made daily expeditions over the Steppes, tasting the new air and bringing back bouquets of spring flowers.

Yet at length one morning at the end of April I slung my travelling-bed across my back and set out to explore.

There are only two regular roads over the Caucasus, and although both start near Vladikavkaz I took neither of them. One goes to Tiflis and the other to Kutais. The former is the well-known Georgian Military Road, the other is a very ill-made, broken track, ascending to an elevation of 9000 feet, and impassable many months of the year.

A brawling river flows past the town from the mountains, the Terek. It is an impetuous, shallow stream that one could almost jump across at some seasons of the year, but having a bed a hundred yards wide. Looking into the valley from the mountains one sees a vast field of grey stones and boulders; and the river, meandering along it, gleams like a silver chain. Sometimes, however, after a few very hot days in July, it rises in flood and covers the whole bed, and washes away bridges and cottages and cattle. The hotter the weather the deeper the water; in June or July it is impossible to ford it, even on a strong horse. It follows that in midwinter it is shallowest and clearest. The Georgian road has been constructed on one side, and there have been several occasions when it has been flooded. There is a number of villages in the valley; it is convenient to be near water. They are inhabited by mountain people, Georgians, Ossetines, Ingooshi. It

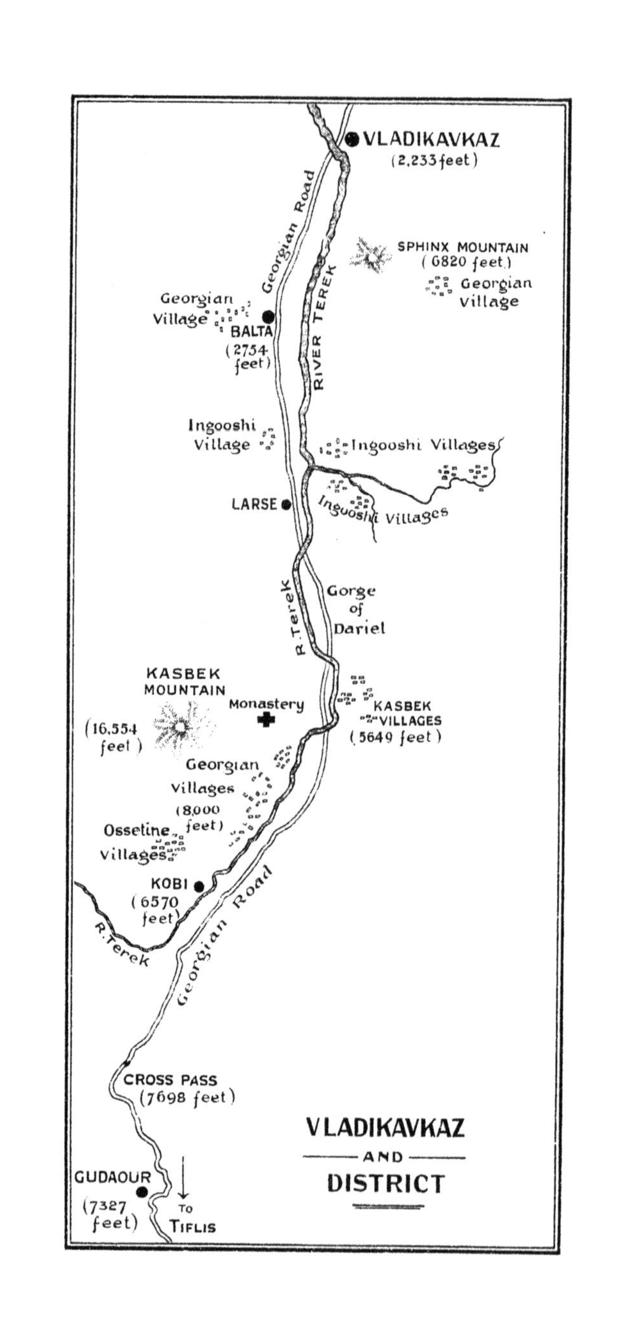
VLADIKAVKAZ
(2,233 feet)
Georgian Road
SPHINX MOUNTAIN
(6820 feet)
Georgian Village
Georgian Village
BALTA
(2754 feet)
RIVER TEREK
Ingooshi Village
Ingooshi Villages
LARSE
Ingooshi Villages
R. Terek
Gorge of Dariel
KASBEK MOUNTAIN
(16,554 feet)
Monastery
KASBEK VILLAGES
(5649 feet)
Georgian Villages
(8,000 feet)
Osseline Villages
KOBI
(6570 feet)
R. Terek
Georgian Road
CROSS PASS
(7698 feet)
GUDAOUR
(7327 feet)
To TIFLIS
VLADIKAVKAZ AND DISTRICT

is strange that villages on opposite banks are near neighbours in the winter, but are cut off from mutual intercourse in the summer. Fortoug, for instance, is half a mile distant from Maximkina in January, but is thirty miles away in June, and both villages are inhabited by the same tribe—Ingooshi. I took the cart track that leads to Fortoug, and thought to be able to cross over to the opposite village. I found out my mistake later on. Mistakes, however, were not going to disturb me. I had no destination. It didn't matter what happened or how far I strayed. The Caucasus was my host; I left him the arrangements. The mountains provided the entertainment, and I would not doubt their hospitality and generosity.

I passed through meadows; they were purple with a little flower which grew in clusters, a labiate, common in England, but incomparably brighter there than here. Early purple orchis was just blossoming, and crimson iris and fig-wort and crane's-bill. In one deep tangled ditch where thistles, barberry, teasle, hollyhock and mallow struggled with nettles and convolvulus, one read the promises for July and August. Nature stood there like a host with drawn bows; in a moment ten thousand arrows would have sped into the air. The orchis and the crane's-bill were heralds. Even the butterflies on the wing were forerunners—tattered old brimstones and tortoiseshells that had lived through the winter, only to wake up in the spring and lay their eggs and prepare the way for their children. And among the birds it was nesting-time; as I climbed a grassy slope I suddenly disturbed a lark, and just at my feet found the little nest with the familiar little cluster of dark eggs.

CHAPTER XIII

A MOUNTAIN DAWN

I HAD turned aside from the track to climb the side of a wooded hill near the Stolovy Mountain; I had an idea that I might find a sheltered spot among the trees. I had not slept out before, and I feared to be found sleeping by any of the natives. I was not a rich prey for the robber, but in Russia they steal even one's clothes. There are many stories current in Vladikavkaz which must have a certain amount of foundation in truth. According to a loquacious cabman I listened to in Vladikavkaz, a coach was stopped one day on the Georgian road, twelve miles outside the town. It contained a pleasure party, a number of ladies and gentlemen out to spend the day, and they were all despoiled of their clothing. The robbers covered them with guns and called on them to undress and throw all their possessions in a heap on the road or be shot. And they accordingly returned to the town in Adam's raiment.

I had one moment of thrills this day. I had just emerged from a wood on to a grassy ridge of the mountain, when I saw a shepherd's camping-ground guarded by dogs. The dogs saw me at the same moment, and all four came tearing along towards me. They were something between bull-dogs and mastiffs, and I had a good mind to climb a tree at once. But something restrained me; the dogs were perhaps too close; I had a cudgel in my hand, I grasped it firmly and awaited the onslaught. Every dog's eye was riveted on my stick, and they all slackened speed suddenly and skirmished to bite at my heels or dart under my arm. They failed and slunk off; they were only uncivilised collies after all. I was relieved. Many a man in my position might have fired a revolver and then the owners of the dogs would have declared war. I recalled the words of Freshfield, the mountaineer, concerning such positions: "It is judicious to avoid petty wrangles with Ossetes and to tranquillise their sheep-dogs with ice-axes rather than to dismiss them with firearms." A shepherd came up to me in a few minutes and began the common series of interrogations—Where do you come from? Where are you going to? Why? What are you—a Russian? I answered him very vaguely that I was going to Dalin-Dalin, a little village near by, on business, and that I was not a Russian. "You ought to be afraid to go in these parts," said he, "many men get killed; a mate of mine was murdered near here last month."

I heard him with a little thrill, but did not alter my plans. I found a bush, and just after sunset, when the gnats sang in their mournful choirs, I made my bed. I was soon deep snuggled in my waterproof sleeping-sack —my dear old friend—night sharer of so many vicissitudes and slumbers. A wisp of *crêpe de chine* about my head, I feared not the meanest of all foes, the mosquitoes that range two to each hair on the hand. I know what happened as the darkness deepened: the birds slunk to sleep in the bushes, all save the night-jars and the owls that gurgled and hooted among the pines and maples. The dark moths flitted to and fro in the first breathless darkness of the summer night, the large red ants carried off on their backs the dead gnats that had perished at my hands at supper-time. Then the pale full moon arose out of a depth of soft white cloud—passionless, perfect. Still the owls hooted as I fell asleep. The night passed. Morning came and I arose gaily. Nought of what the hill-man suggested had come to pass; only once I had started, and that at the touch of the wet snout of an inquisitive hedgehog. I remember now how piggy scuttled off. But two minutes after that I was sleeping again. There had been one other event of the night. About two hours before dawn the rain came softly down. A broad cloud had gently breasted this little mountain upon which I was encamped. It rained steadily and much. I curled myself more completely within my sack and let it rain. In the little moments when I did not sleep I heard the drops falling on the cover above me. Had any wild robber come upon this strange bundle under the bush his woodlore must have told him it was no beast or bird ever seen upon the hills or under the sky. I think he would have crossed himself and passed by.

So passed my first night of my tramp in the mountains, quite a unique night, soft, strange, wonderful. I felt I had begun a new life. I had entered into a new world and come into communion with Nature in a way as yet unknown.

The rain had stopped as the first light came up into the sky. I arose gaily, pleasantly cool and fit after the sleep and the rain. By the faint light I saw the valley below me, and the grand grey rocks on the other side. I looked up to the summit of my own mountain, and as I munched a remainder of dry bread felt all the unspeakable delight of an awakening with the birds after having spent the night with the mountains. But, indeed, I had awakened before the birds, and as yet the mountains slept, the long grey line of bearded warriors, calm, majestic, unmoved, invincible. Nature in reverence lay hushed beneath them, waiting for a signal. I passed carefully over the wet grasses—softly, secretly, as if everywhere children slept.

Clamber, clamber, clamber, up then to the highest point. At last I stood there with the dew on my heels. All the east lay before me, and such a horizon as one can only see when looking from the northern spurs of the Caucasus. The sun had not risen, and from north to south lay an illimitable length of deep blood red, blood without life, red without light—dead, fearful, unfathomable red. I stood as one convicted, as a too-daring one, awe-stricken. From the place where I had slept I had not dreamed of this; no tinge on the morning twilight had suggested what the obstacle of the peak withheld. I felt pale and grey as a morning mist, insubstantial as a shadow. The grasses trembled wet at my feet. Behind me the austere mountains sat unmoved, deep in undisturbed sleep or contemplation. No bird sang, no beast moved, not even the wet trees dripped. All waited for a signal, and I waited. Death was passed—life not come. I was at the gates of the day, but had come early. . . .

I was looking westward when the world awoke, looking at the grey mountains. Suddenly it was as if they blushed. Crimson appeared in a valley and ran and spread along the cliffs and rocks and over chasms, suffusing the whole westward scene. It was the world blushing as the first kiss of the sun awakened it to a new day. And as I turned, there in the west was the hero, raising himself unaided victoriously upward. It was the sun, the hot, glorious one, uprising, glistening, burning out of a sea of scarlet, changing the blood into ruby and firing every raindrop to a diamond. Most glorious it was, seen, as it were, by one alone, and that one myself, upon a peak adding my few feet to its five thousand and taking also that crimson reflection, that rosette or favour accorded those presented at the opening of the day. At how many town pageants had one been a mocker, but here was ritual that stood majestic, imperious in its meaning—only to be revered.

The ceremony was at length over. The day was opened, the freedom of the world had been given, one had but to step down into the gardens laid open to man.

Down the hill and over a moor the way led to the little red-roofed village called Dalin-Dalin. Ten steep downhill miles they were, and every mile waved invitingly. Onward then downward, and with steady steps, for the rain has left everything slippery. Wet it is, wet, and the grasses and fern and scrub are up to the waist, but the sun will dry both these and me, and by noon we shall all be hot and thirsty. Through a long wood the path goes. Last week, when I was in the woods, the ground was golden with cowslips, but the fairies' pensioners are now all gone. Only the tall tiger lilies look down like modest maidens, and brown-green-fingered ferns hold out little monkey hands. Wet, wet —in the boots the water squirts and squeezes. A hare pauses in front and then bounces off—the long-legged, easy runner. So steep and wet is the path that it is difficult to keep one's footing, and one has to hold on to the branches to keep balance. Mile after mile the distance gets accomplished, and the wood is passed. Beyond the wood is a valley of nettles, immense docks, waste comfrey, canterbury bells and entwined convolvulus, such a bed of rank vegetable as only the black virgin earth, the mountain mist and hot noonday sun can bring forth. Through that! There is even country ahead and less chance of snakes. Yonder the wild rose blooms and the eglantine and snowy guelder rose. The sun is getting hotter, and half-dazed flies wake to a morrow they had not expected; they buzz stupidly at one's nose and ears—they have some stale news to impart. It is morning again, they say.

Here is Dalin-Dalin. Just outside the village a dead horse lies on the moor, and the flies fluster about it. Was it killed in some night affray with robbers, I wonder?

The mountains lie peacefully in the sunshine. The birds sing; myriadfold humming and stirring and chirping is in the grass. The rose bushes are daintily apparelled, and tall spurge lifts its yellow face to look at the beauties around. Sleeping in the copse, even in more abundance than yesterday, are next month's flowers: time and the sun are softly wooing them. A few mallow and lily and rose will have faded away and given place to new revellers, new festivities. The morning sun, warmer every moment, promises for to-morrow, to-morrow week, to-morrow month, the blooming of the poppy and the ripening of the vine.

CHAPTER XIV

AMONG THE INGOOSHI

I

AT Dalin-Dalin an old crone served me with sushky biscuits and milk. Her shop had apparently been built to suit her own height, for there was not room for a man to stand up. It was an interesting little shop, and it kept everything, from ink to mushrooms. A large notice on the counter confronted the customer. It said, " No Bargaining," which was very surprising, and suggested to my mind that the owner might have some connection with Germans, for whoever heard of such a sordid notice being put up in a Russian shop. A Georgian horseman had interpreted for me, because the old woman understood no Russian. The Georgian, who was just such a dandy as I have described earlier, was drinking cranberry beer at the table with me and had bought a packet of tea. He had evidently come from a small village where there was no shop; his horse was tied to a post outside. He had given a six-shilling note to change, and all the while we drank the old woman was hunting for coin. I looked on with some amusement, for she had already a large Russian basin full of black, greasy coppers. She began counting them out very seriously. I put a question through the Georgian, asking if she had any eggs in the shop. When it had been repeated, she looked up for a moment and replied: no, but she would go out and find some. And she lost count and said something which seemed to correspond to " Eh, deary, deary, deary, dear." Then suddenly her husband, an old gaffer, came in, and deposited a little bag of three-farthing bits, about a hundred of them. So they made up the change, all of coppers, though the horseman expostulated, " All that black money even a strong horse couldn't carry! "

The tribe that inhabits Dalin-Dalin is the Ingoosh, said to be descended from Englishmen, hence their name. An idea is current that the Crusaders used to go to the Holy Land by the old Georgian road, which for two thousand years has been the one recognised road over the Caucasus. A number of English were converted to Mahommedanism and settled in the mountains and took Caucasian women to wife. Their language has many words reminiscent of English, but I think the legend rather an unlikely story. It compares favourably with the myth that the Georgians are descended from the Egyptian army of Sesostris, who marched into the Caucasus and disappeared from their native land for ever more. And both stories find a companion in the explanation the priests give to the peasants that it was in the Caucasus that the Tower of Babel was built, the Babylonian Steeple, as they call it, and that the hundred different races and languages are the living proof of the confusion of tongues.

Just outside the village an Ingoosh chief rode up to me. He was a fine figure. He sat erect on a black horse; on his shoulder hung a black sheepskin cloak, his breast was ornamented by silver-mounted cartridge cases; at his belt of polished leather were pistol and dagger. A scimitar in a silver sheath lay across the shoulders of his horse and was attached to his belt by a light chain. His brows and hair were bushy and black, his eyes keen and domineering. He held the reins with one hand and kept wheeling his horse about. He was evidently in wrath and indignation; his aspect boded terror. I spoke first and greeted him.

"Hail!"

"Hail! Where are you from?"

"Dalin-Dalin."

"Where are you going to?"

"The next village."

"What do you mean?"

"The next village; I don't know what it is called."

"Why?"

"To see it."

"That's not the truth. Besides, there is no next village. You must go back."

INGOOSH WOMEN, WITH WATER-JAR

" Yes, all right, afterwards."

" Afterwards! What do you mean? I say *at once!* "

" Yes? "

" Yes. What is your tribe? You're not a Russian? "

" I am an Englishman."

" A what? That's not true. . . . The English travel in flying-machines."

I convinced him by showing my passport,whereupon he was much mollified and begged me to do him the honour of sleeping under his roof that night. I said that if I could not get forward I would return and take advantage of his hospitality. So we parted. I never went back.

I knew he was without authority, and that the dapper little Russian officials in Vladikavkaz had three times his power. Though one would say they were but thirds of men, pitiable waste ends of men beside this proud cavalier, yet he was more amenable to the common law than they were. A hundred years ago would he not have been a king and they—slaves! But the wheel of fortune has turned.

The road onward was lined with the tombs of chiefs. I had walked about three miles before I came to the first of these; each grave was marked by a high stone, on which was represented, in red and blue painting, the estate of the deceased. The stones stood upright, because they marked the graves of Mahommedans; the tombstones of Christians lie flat on the ground. The name and fame of the deceased was set forth in characters resembling Georgian or Persian writing, and all around the writing were little paintings of the different things that marked him out as a nobleman—his swords, daggers, pistols, his belt and scimitar. Above the writing was shown the moon under which he died, and the star or stars. And underneath the writing and the martial emblems were little pictures of his domestic belongings, of his tea-kettle and his water-jar and his praying beads, gently and carefully drawn so that one loved mankind for the little dearnesses there. The painter had actually put in his goloshes and his jack-boots and the rug he slept on. On this first tomb, too, it was all arranged in the shape of a man; the moon represented his head, the stars his neck, the swords his arms, the jack-boots his feet, and the writing in the middle his body. It seemed to me that men had tried to gain the attention of God and had done this like children, wishing to be taken notice of. If there is a human God that comprehends our life He must smile at our dear ways. Man must be very lovable to Him.

I walked by many tombs and all were similarly marked; some were larger than others, and had many stones around for the traveller to rest upon. I took rest at noon and ate my mid-day meal and looked upon the scene. Near by, on a ridge, there were graves of another sort, a close-packed cemetery with hundreds of stones, and on them no emblems were painted and no names written. They were the graves of the retainers, of the nameless many. Six miles away, on a mountain, I saw the village of Fortoug. Thence the way wound indolently upward along the sides of gnarled cliffs. A thousand feet beneath lay the silver river. The scene was one of splendour and of strange, wild beauty. For a moment I was alone with myself. It seemed that the wild earth that is so shy of men had taken me to herself and had lost all her timidity. She was living as she does when no one is looking on. Earth is more beautiful than all women, more gentle than the timidest, more splendid than the grandest. . . . A pathos of longing came over me as if a cloud had crept into the sky; I was solitary; why was I here? What was happening in the other places of the world, in Moscow, in Lisitchansk, in London, on Ludgate Hill, in my English home? Why did man live in a scene and forget all the other scenes that existed at the same time? Why did I long to be conscious of the whole surface of life at once, to be, as it were, everywhere at home at once? The pathos of the present time is that it is breadth with length, infinite breadth, and that our scene is only one point on that infinite line. The Present Time is everywhere at once. Its duration is but for an instant, a minute, an hour, but its content is universal. It is more instant than light shed, it covers the worlds at once and is existent simultaneously to the ends of space, and it is as punctual on the furthest star as on the little mountain road where I am sitting. The blade of grass trembling at my feet has trembled just in time. Its movement is contemporaneous with the present time all over the world. The shadow which for a moment dwells over the valley, changing the little mountain rivulet which is tumbling down to the Terek from a warm, flashing, inviting stream to what appears a river of salt or ice, is the aspect of the present time made up for me by the gnarled and frowning cliffs, the mountain road, the heavy ox-cart upon it and the clumsy, patient oxen beating up the dust, the ruined castle on the mountain, with the cottages of Fortoug clinging to it like lichen, and the clustered gravestones on the knoll where the tribesmen lie buried, and the solitary tombs of the chiefs. It is made up for God, the universal eye, by—everything!

At Fortoug the whole village turned out to see me, and the old man of the place took charge of me and sat me in his best room whilst his daughter made dinner for me. And he had never seen an Englishman before, had never heard of them, the Inglechani, for that was how he translated the Russian word Anglichanin into his language. Where did my tribe lie? He was surprised not to have seen any of us in their valley before. I pointed north-west, beyond Elbruz. He nodded as if he understood, and then my meal came up—lamb cutlet and millet-bread—bread baked of millet-seed and very dry. Then the old gentleman showed me photographs of his four sons, fine fellows; they had all left home and gone he knew not where. He begged me to remain and rest as long as I pleased, and assured me I could find no further road into the mountains, and that the river was unfordable, and that I should have to return the way I came.

As I did not wish to rest or to take his advice about the road I thought it better to pretend I would return to Dalin-Dalin. That satisfied him. It did not occur to him that I should make a detour and follow the river course, path or no path.

II

As the sun was sinking I found a resting-place soon. I chose a pleasant grassy hollow sheltered by two boulders. It was above the road and just beneath a graveyard: I could see all that happened on the road without standing the chance of being seen myself. But in truth there was little to see, beyond an occasional horseman and an ox-cart now and then. Each man who came rested a little beside the tombs before going on, for the road was a stiff climb. At sunset a party of Mahommedans came and said their prayers, faced Mecca, bowed to the earth, kissed it, rose and bowed again.

Then the owls stepped out from their hiding-places in the walls of the rocks and flew for little stretches noiselessly, and shrieked at one another. The shadow after sunset had begun low and now was claiming the summits of the cliffs; presently it would rest upon the sky itself, and night would have come. One by one the stars appeared, and I lay in my sleeping-sack and looked up at them. It became a perfect night, lit by a bright moon and a myriad of clearest stars. There was a silent breeze and a freshness on its wings; I lay full stretched on the ground and fitted my body to the soft earth. One could almost imagine that the dead in the tombs all lay as I did and stared into the starry heaven: I looked at the railed-in village of the dead above me and down to where the large tombs lay. They did lie as the poet wished, " under the wide and starry sky," and, to the dwellers in the villages, to be buried so was ordinary. They knew of no other life or death. They could not compare their stars with other stars, and therefore knew not of their beauty. I had seen the human stars lit on the Thames Embankment. It seemed very beautiful that the hand which wrote:

> " Under the wide and starry sky
> Dig the grave and let me lie,"

also wrote, " There are no stars like the Edinburgh gas-lamps and no atmosphere like the air of Auld Reekie." Again one wished to be everywhere at home. " Philosophy," Novalis said, " was home-sickness."

A little procession of cloud-scuds passed over the sky and I fell asleep. I awakened again as the dawn light was flooding upward: the peaks of distant white summits were rosy-red with the reflection of sunrise. Then gradually, as the shadow had climbed upward the night before, so the light came down—down, down into the valley. It was as if angels were being let down by shining rope ladders. A lark jumped from the grass beside me, brown and wet, and twittered on a boulder and sang three notes. It was magical.

I gathered sticks and dry grass and made a fire, and watched it burn, and boiled a kettle on it, and made tea and munched millet-bread. I had a supply of this "biscuit." After tea a river dip and then onward!

The whole of this day, from sunrise to sunset, I wandered and met not one human being. Therefore I nearly starved, for I had a very poor day's rations in my bag. After making my detour past Fortoug I had to climb the steep cliff in order to proceed, for there was no means of following the river otherwise. The water hugged the rock and was very deep and rapid. I crept through a wood on hands and knees, and when I got to the other side found an impassable wall stretching up to the snow-line. I found a cleft, however, and a path leading away from the direction I wished to take. I went along this. It was difficult to follow, and led up to a perfectly barren region, where there was not a shrub or blade of grass, or even a piece of moss to be seen; nothing but grey rock and the waste end of last winter's snow, not yet melted by the summer sun. I grew rather anxious, for I had no wish to sleep at such a height in such cold air, but suddenly the path diverged downward again, and late in the evening I clambered down a dangerously steep slope right into a valley. The boulders were very loose, and there was a chaos of them, large and small. One had to step from one to another all the way down, and sometimes just a touch would send a rock bigger than myself thundering into the valley below. At last, in the twilight of the evening, I found myself on the Georgian road in the Gorge of Dariel. I was some way up the gorge, just at the Transcaucasian frontier. I hailed a cart coming along and got a lift to the Kazbek village. It was quite dark when we arrived, so I plucked out Nicholas's epistle from my bosom and inquired the way to the village pope.

CHAPTER XV

THE IKON NOT MADE BY HANDS

VLADIMIR ALEXANDROVITCH was, I suppose, one of the minor clergy. It was evident he was very poor; his house consisted of one room only, and was furnished by two chairs and a table. Several Ikons hung on the walls. On the floor a rough black sheepskin mat showed where he slept. He wouldn't find me a lodging, but bade me welcome to his own. We ate *kasha* together, buckwheat porridge, and then he put the samovar on and we had tea. The Ikons were all Christ-faces, and they watched us all through the meal in a way that gave the place a strange atmosphere. At my elbow stood a famous picture, one that many Russians love beyond all others as a comforter. It is called " The Joy of all the Afflicted "; it is, of course, a portrait of Christ painted in the features of a Russian peasant. It means nothing to a foreigner, but somehow it appeals to the peasant; it brings Christ very near to him, it makes Him a fellow-man. Opposite me was " The Ikon not made by hands," also a peasant face, but having an expression as cold as the other was warm.

But this one was arresting; one's eyes continually rested upon it and tried to discover some hidden meaning. I asked the priest to tell me the story of it, and it was not until the end that I discovered that it was a version of the St Veronica legend. I don't know now whether he would agree with the version of his story I should tell. But this is how it remains in my mind.

The fame of Jesus spread into many countries, even before the time of His death. It came to Abyssinia where a queen was dying. The tidings came of the healing of the sick, the raising from the dead, tidings of all the wonderful faith-miracles wrought in the distant land where Jesus was teaching. The tidings were brought to the dying queen, and as she heard a light passed over her face. All those who stood by wondered and hoped, for in the sudden light in the eyes of the queen they deemed they saw the promise of new life. The queen was silent, and looked on them, and then the light faded away, and she said: "If I might see Him it is possible I should live, but how could it happen that He should come hither, so many hundred miles o'er hill and vale and desert and sea, for the sake even of a queen?" So she spoke and was silent, and yet was not without hope. And those around her were sad, and they waited for the queen to say more. But the queen lay still and spoke no more, and with a strange thought of comfort her feeble body and spirit slid gently into sleep. Sweetly and gently her eyes and soul closed to the day, and her night eyes and soul opened to the night. She dreamed. She dreamed, and then even her dreaming self fell asleep.

In the morning she opened her eyes and remembered that she had dreamed, and she remembered a voice in the dream, and a face and a promise. She remembered the strange words that had been spoken to her dreaming self—" Andray, the painter, shall bring you the face that shall save you from all harm."

The queen bade heralds sound for Andray, the painter. They sounded, and a painter, Andray by name, was found, and they brought him before the queen. Then, when he was come, and he stood before the pale queen, she told him the purport of the dream, and told him of the tidings of that Jesus of Galilee whose comfort her soul craved. Andray understood his quest—that he should paint the face—and that day, ere the sun set, he departed on his long journey. His long travelling commenced. Far over hill and vale and sea and desert he journeyed to the Holy Land, there to see the Saviour and paint the face that should save the queen.

And a high faith held the pale queen between life and death during the intervening weeks, and a kindred faith bore Andray through hardship and peril and the fear of man and of beast. The commotion and stir and rumour with regard to the Saviour grew noisier as Andray came nearer Palestine. At length he arrived.

Jesus was teaching among the people, living in His heart the life of everyone He saw, living from His heart in living veins over the whole earth. Of the queen He knew in His heart, and of her faith, and of the painter and his faith, and He in His own heart had the fulfilment of each, the answer to each. And as part of that answer, on the day on which Andray arrived, He stood upon a slope teaching, and below Him were a thousand people, listening, calling, reviling, praying, and the disciples were bringing sick people to and fro at the Master's feet. So great was the crowd that Andray found it impossible to get near, or he was too tired to struggle through. So he climbed the opposite hill, that which faced the one whereon Jesus was working, for the people were in a valley between two hills. And from that eminence Andray had a perfect view of the face that he needed to paint.

So the painter settled down to make his study, and he found the face such a subject as he had never yet imagined, such a face as was only one with his highest dream of an ideal, one with the fleeting fancy of the golden moment of his greatest love. Eagerly he drew—eagerly for a moment—and then stopped in perplexity. There was something wrong; he put aside his first attempt and eagerly started a second. But the second also he put aside, and started a third; and a fourth and a fifth he started, for he found that directly he traced a line it was wrong. The slightest feature that he drew seemed at once a lie. For the living face of the Teacher changed constantly, like the flash of the sun on the waves; it was not one face only that he saw, but a thousand faces; not a thousand faces only, but every face, and even for a moment his own face.

Jesus knew that he was there, and had marked him where he sat at work upon the opposite hill. And now He beckoned to him, and Andray gave up his efforts and made his way down the slope. Then one of the disciples found him at the edge of the crowd and brought him to the throng, to the place where Jesus was teaching. And when he was brought Jesus looked at him and said, " My face may not be drawn by hands, lest in the days to come man should say *this only* is the likeness of Christ. There is not one face alone for all, but for each man his own vision. There is one common knowledge for all, *that* only the heart may know. What wouldest thou then? "

" I would that I had the likeness that alone can save my queen."

Then Jesus took a towel and pressed it to His face, and then gave it to Andray. And on the towel was imprinted a strange likeness of Christ. And all who looked upon the picture marvelled, for there was in it portraiture such as never painter's hand could follow. And Andray gazed, rapt, upon the living, breathing treasure that was his, and he marvelled at the depth and plenitude of power and love that breathed from its unfathomable calm; it seemed a myriad souls were merged in one face. And he looked questioningly at the thorn crown upon the head and the blood marks on the brow, for in such guise was the face portrayed. There was much in the picture that was as yet hidden from his heart.

This was the face that Andray, the painter, brought from Palestine, which restored to life the pale queen, and which, set in the holy seat of the capital, wrought many wonders and miracles. It is told that Andray, though his paintings are now lost, became the most wonderful painter, and his fame went throughout the land; for before taking away the Ikon of Christ he had received a blessing. At parting Jesus breathed on the eyes of the painter, and said, "Thou couldest not find My face for the reflection there of the soul of the common man. Behold now, thou shalt not look upon the face of any common man but thou shalt find My face there also."

I liked the priest's legend and probably read much more in it than he intended. Indeed, he seemed mildly surprised at my enthusiastic inquiries as to points in the story. Shortly after he concluded the lamp burned out, and as he had no more oil we went to bed. And I slept very soundly, for I had had a stiff day's walk, and had not slept particularly well since I left Vladikavkaz.

Next day I was awakened by the sun full in my face. It was time to go out. I left the priest fast asleep and went out to see the Kazbek Mountain. The air was so cold that it was necessary to run to keep warm even though the sun shone. There was mist on the mountains and the sun was fighting it. Far distant peaks looked immense and elemental, like chaotic heaps awaiting the creation of a world. And the conquering sun was creating all things anew, and momentarily all around me the gems of the earth were, as it were, answering *adsum* to the morning roll-call. Hyacinth and iris glittering with dew crept out of the wet scrub and gleamed in the sunlight, and fritillary butterflies came flitting down upon the blossoms.

Then above me rose the majestic mountain to which in old time Prometheus, as the story goes, was bound, Mount Caucasus, the wonder of the way. Its high-born pinnacle of snow seemed to have riven the very sky itself, and was all glistering white, as if catching the radiance of another world. Mount Kazbek seemed a god; the other mountains were men. The other mountains were like grandfathers, hoary old men who wanted children playing at their knees. They enticed me. Grandfathers are very fond of their children's children.

CHAPTER XVI

AT A MILL ON THE TEREK

THE yard cocks are at feud. There has been some harem trouble and so this is a day of war. Since first crow they have been tumbling over one another, shedding the red gore and eyeing one another terribly. Now, at four of the afternoon, they both show signs of strife. Their grand plumage is dirty, their combs soiled and ugly, their necks gory, their eyes bloodshot and terrible. Their wives, however, seem placid—almost indifferent. Unhappy is the lot of rival Sultans!

There are intervals between the battles, intervals of rest and crowing. Poor Abdul Hamid sits below me and groans with pain, whines almost like a dog. But in a minute " time's up," he goes out and challenges and again is bloodily overcome. Their claws are bloody, for they strike at one another with their feet. They jump at one another, balancing themselves and flapping their wings and try to roll each other in the dust. Truly it is no wonder there is cock-fighting in Russia when the birds behave like this when left to themselves.

KAZBEK MOUNTAIN, FROM THE NORTH-WEST

And it is a most interesting spectacle albeit not Christian.

Whilst they are eyeing one another terribly and furtively, and it looks doubtful whether Abdul will continue the battle or will abdicate, Alimka, the yard urchin, steals up behind the victor and suddenly pulls one of his tail feathers. Consternation! But in a moment they are back again, beak to beak, and the ruby blood is flowing. A black hen is now in attendance, and risks having her eyes pecked out in her greedy endeavours to drink up the blood that is dropping on the ground.

This is happening in the yard of a mill where I am staying. I came here yesterday in a cart from the mountains, and I have given up the quest of a cottage for this summer. I have taken two rooms here, and although they are unfurnished they will suit my purposes. It is on the banks of the Terek, and presently I shall have to go to the river to fetch water for tea.

I had been wandering some days among the Georgian villages near Kobi, when one morning I came into the Georgian Road again and there met a Russian driving a three-horse cart. He seemed badly in want of company, so I consented to get in with him. We had the following conversation.

"How do you pray?" asked he.

"What do you mean?" I replied.

"Are you orthodox?"

"I am not Russian," I replied, "and I don't belong to the Russian church."

"What then? You are Esthonian, ėh? Or a Tsech?"

"No, English."

"English! Impossible! You have a moustache, no Englishman has a moustache."

"I am English all the same."

"Then you are a Protestant. I'm a Baptist."

"Then we are brothers," I replied.

"But how do you pray? Do you cross yourself? We pray so." He showed me how he prayed, folded his hands on his stomach, and shut his eyes.

"I understand," I replied. "We pray like that, but we kneel also, and some of our Protestants cross themselves also."

He looked shocked but went on:

"Where do you live? You ought to come to our gatherings. There are many of us here now since the Declaration."

He was referring to M. Stolypin's Ukase of October 1908, which granted freedom to all religious sects in the Empire. I told him I was not living anywhere in particular, but that I had been tempted to take a Georgian cottage at a place called Pkhelshi, which had been offered me at ten roubles a month. My only doubt was of the cleanliness of the place. I was afraid of being eaten up by insects. The Baptist was horrified.

"Afraid of insects!" said he. "Better be afraid of getting your throat cut. No, you leave it to me; I know where you can go. I'll take you to our pastor, he has a mill on the river. He is a very good man and very humble. You go and live with him, he won't take more than five roubles."

So I had come to the mill and put my things there, and made it my abode for the time being. The driver of the cart was very proud of his find, and introduced me to the miller with not less mystery and secrecy than he would have unwrapped a gold nugget which he might have picked up on the mountains. The host took me over and the other bade me farewell; we should meet again at one of their "gatherings."

I had two rooms but no furniture. The miller found me a table and I used a box to sit on. I bought a mattress at a "bazaar" in Vladikavkaz, and a German oil-stove and glasses and saucers and plates and a saucepan, and a wooden spoon to stir my soup, and metal spoons to eat it and sup it, and some knives and a fork. I also bought a penny broom to sweep the floors and some muslin to make a curtain. Setting up house on my own account for the first time was a matter of great excitement. In case anyone might like to try a similar experiment let me write here the prices I paid:

Mattress	6 shillings
Oil-stove (of the Beatrice kind) . .	7 „
2 buckets	2 „
2 saucers, 4 plates, 2 glasses . . .	1 „
Saucepan	2 „
Tea-pot and hot-water jug . . .	1 „
A broom, padlock, nails . . .	1 „
A shopping-basket	6 pence

and the muslin cost 8d., and two tins for washing purposes cost 1s. 6d. The other people were very interested in my place, but did not seem surprised at the deficiencies. A Russian woman promised to do my washing, and my neighbour, a Persian, offered me water from his samovar whenever I required it.

It was an interesting *ménage*, and left me free to go out into the mountains whenever I wished. I could leave my things behind and be perfectly sure they were safe, and I could have a postal address. Food cost me about four shillings a week—for the cost of living was very low. Milk was 2d. a quart; new-laid eggs, 3d. a dozen; butter, 10d. a pound; lamb, 4d. a pound; beef, 3d. I lived on the fat of the land at four shillings a week, and on very hot days I would take my saucepan out to the ice-cream shop and get it full for sixpence, and then I would invite Alimka, the yard urchin, and his little sister, Fatima, to have tea with me.

One day Fatima and Alimka brought me a sparrow

which they had caught. They had tied cotton to one of its legs and had been flying it as one would a kite. They did not understand cruelty; they thought I should be amused. So when I took it away they were fearfully enraged, and I offered them each a halfpenny, and Alimka took his, but Fatima would not take it; she would have the sparrow back, it was *hers*. She screamed, and I thought she was going to have a fit. "*Daviety*," she screamed, "give it back," and put everything into that scream—mouth, face, head, feet, knees, body and red rag of a skirt; all shook and gaped and screamed, "*Daviety*." She did not have her way, however, and little Jason, for so I named him, remained with me, and many a cheerful hour we spent together. For days I amused myself watching his convalescence. I caught flies for him and put them in his mouth, whereupon he gulped them down and chirped. He slept every night on the winter stove, and in the mornings he flew down and hopped on to my face and chirped, and then I would waken up and give him some sugar. I took him out and he hopped along at the side of me on the moors, and jumped and flew and caught flies for himself. Often he got lost and I could not find him, but after an hour or so, when I was lying down eating my lunch, or picking wild strawberries from a bank, he would hop again into view. He was a dear friend, my little Jason.

Of wild strawberries I made jam, as also of wild

plums and cherries, and this was a great diversion. I offered some to Ali Khan next door, but he would not take any; perhaps it was part of his religion to refuse, for the jam was very tempting. Ali Khan made the Persians very interesting to me, especially as there were many Persians about and he was having one to tea almost every day.

The miller and his wife looked upon me with parental eyes. They were much astonished by my ability to do things for myself. The miller was generally known as the Hözain and his wife the Hözaika. The Hözaika stood and stared at me when I drew water from the river myself; she thought it not respectable that a man should do that, and when she came into my back room one day and found me washing handkerchiefs she fairly gasped. Poor Hözaika, she also had her tables of conventionalities.

CHAPTER XVII

THE GORGE OF DARIEL

LIVING in towns is enervating; it starves both gods and devils. There the half-gods of wit and conversation hold sway. One morning I put a sovereign in my pocket, slung my travelling bed over my shoulder, and resolved to see more of the mountains. The sovereign was in small change.

It was a dull, showery day, and the green trees clung to the mountain sides like soft plumage. I walked the whole day along the Georgian road and met no more than two people beyond the little crowd packed into the stage-coach. In the afternoon I entered the *débris* of Larse, where the famous road enters the great mountains, and I slept in the post-station within sight of the great Ermolovsky stone, famous for its size, and for a Russian poem which it inspired.

Next morning I felt that my journey had begun. For I was at the mouth of the Dariel Gorge. Two versts from the station was the little red bridge which clasps together the great rocks on either bank of the Terek. They call it, as was, I suppose, almost inevitable, the Devil's Bridge, and it looks enchanted. It is overhung by gigantic cliffs, the great walls of the corridor of the gorge. The river which rushes underneath is something incomparably stronger than the bridge itself; it is a monster wallowing, plunging, roaring, thundering, lifting up a hundred dirty heads. No horse or man would stand a chance in its current; even the great glacial boulders, weighing tons, are rolled over and over by its waves, and, shutting one's eyes, one listens to an uproar as of the heaviest streetful of traffic on Cheapside.

I think May is the best time to see the gorge, of a morning at dawn. I was there before the sun had risen. It was then indeed what a Russian has called it, "A fairy tale in twelve versts." There is little verdure there except the grass, but the tops of the cliffs are snow-crested, and just below the snow one sees, far away, the hoar-frosted tops of woods. Below that are two or three thousand feet of rock, brown with withered grass, but brightened here and there by the greenest fir trees. At the base the tortured rock seems wrought in cyphers and frescoes, all twisted and lined as if a great history had been told in hieroglyphics and letters that only some past civilisation had been able to understand. But, as someone has said, "Odin has engraved runes upon all visible things—a divine alphabet intelligible only to the thinking spirit."

The cliffs are crowned here and there by the ruins of

old towers, and the castle of Queen Tamara still stands, a grim survival from the twelfth century when many crimes were accomplished there. One still sees the stairway in the rock along which unfortunate victims used to be taken to be hurled into the foaming river. Even below the ruins the clefts hold snow, and one sees a rivulet of snow and ice descending to become a cascade of bright water. From the river to the sky the whole is harmonised by moss and lichen and ancient greyness. It is a place where the stupendous majesty of Nature troubles the soul, where one feels oppressed by the immanence of powers greater than oneself, where one knows in one's heart how small and feeble is the little earth-born creature Man beside those powers which have fashioned the Universe and which move in the fire-hearts of worlds.

I sat on a stone and looked up. The perfectly blue sky was spread across like a roof. The sun had risen, but would not shine in upon me for hours. Meanwhile I watched the light descending from the mountains, and the sharp shadow picture of the rocks on my side thrown on the rocks of the other. The shadow was gradually climbing down.

How clearly all sounds can be distinguished there! The rocks preserve even the whisper. I notice that when one comes out of the open into the shelter of a gorge all sounds are trebled in volume and in distinctness. One becomes aware of the music of the wind, the roar of the distant torrent; even the little rivulets trickling down from the snow-drifts have a voice that reaches the ear. The waterfalls have two voices, the first a roar, and the second which the listener hears as a secret treble.

I walked on uphill past the boundary line into Trans-Caucasia, past the Government fort and the first free wine-inn of the new territory—the Russians have allowed the vodka monopoly to lapse in Trans-Caucasia—and came to the Devdorak glacier with its long file of snow and ice. Here there was a large pile of snow on the road, hard, firm snow six feet deep. It had dropped from the heights. I walked on top of it, and it was so hard that I did not even make footprints. A man would stand a bad chance against a falling drift.

At Devdorak is the Alexandrovsky Bridge, and I crossed the Terek once more and came to the sunny side of the gorge. A hot sun shone and a bracing wind rushed round the corners of the serpentine road. Butterflies purple and brown disported themselves, and where the water oozed through the porphyry the rocks were festooned with flowers.

DARIEL GORGE: CASTLE OF QUEEN TAMARA AND RUSSIAN FORTRESS

CHAPTER XVIII

AT A VILLAGE INN

OUTSIDE Kazbek village two sheep-dogs came up with a great show of ferocity, but I pacified them. I have discovered that they only do this because they are starved, and that if one aims them a bit of bread they become like lambs. The natives' practice is perhaps more efficacious. They pick up as big a piece of rock as they can find, and hurl it point blank at the beast's head. I only counsel the reader, should he find himself in such a predicament and not have bread, to offer them a stone.

I slept the night at the post-station at Kobi. Next morning, when I went out to an inn to get some tea, it was snowing, which rather surprised me, seeing that the day before had been so hot.

The inn is one of eight shops in Kobi. The inn-keeper was of course delighted to see me. A customer in May is a rarity. I had hardly seated myself when a Russian lounger pounced on me and asked me the usual series of questions about my name, nationality, destination, business and so forth. He was dressed in home-made sheepskin trousers and a Russian national shirt.

"Ah," said he, "the Englishmen know where all the gold and copper is, and the oil; they've got it all mapped out. The English know all. The Russians keep all—that, my friend, is politics. The Caucasus is the brightest brilliant in the Russian crown. We shall keep it to the last. When all the rest is worked out we shall begin. Here there is everything: gold, silver, coal, copper, iron—what you like. Why, I know villages where there is wild petroleum; it spurts out naturally, and the natives have used it for years for cooking and lighting. Here at Kobi we have seltzer water so strong that no one can bottle it, and we drink it by the pailful. Full of iron, my friend, that's what makes us all strong. Nobody ever dies here; that's because of our springs."

Whilst I was having my tea I got him to speak of the road. He was evidently a chatterbox.

"They spend ten thousand roubles a year on the road," said he. "But that is nearly all absorbed by overseers and generals; the poor working men get little."

"That also is politics," said I.

"Yes, we are all very poor," put in the innkeeper. "Eight shops we have, and not one makes more than threepence a day profit. You see we have eight months winter."

"It will be better soon," I urged. "The summer

is coming. But I see you don't know much about business. Now I know comparatively little about trade, but my little finger knows better than you do how to manage a shop like this."

The shopkeeper blinked his eyes; he was an Ossetine. Then the little man in the sheepskin trousers broke in, "You would like to introduce American methods, but you don't understand how poor they are. They never have any money in the winter. You couldn't get change for a rouble in the whole village now. They spend all they get in the summer, and live on credit all the winter. They owe you a fortune, Achmet, I'll be bound."

"It is only too true," assented the shopkeeper.

The little man went on: "Why, they even buy two calf-skins of wine in the autumn when they have money, and that lasts the family through the winter. Not even an Englishman could do trade here."

"Well," I said, "what I meant was, soon the summer will be here, and crowds of Georgians and Armenians, Russians and Persians will be on the road. Now, this being the first shop in the village, it stands best chance. But why does our friend call the inn a drapery establishment, and fill his window with oil-lamps and cheese?"

The shopkeeper smiled with pride, and pointed out that he was the only draper and lamp-seller in the village. Whereupon I went on instructing him.

"If you are the only draper, then everyone in the

village knows that fact, and there is no need to paint it up as your sign. But travellers don't want to buy drapery or lamps. What you need to do is to write up in big letters,

INN

VARIOUS DRINKS

WINE

SAMOVAR READY

HOT SOUP.

Then you'd make more than threepence a day. You ought to try and get Russian visitors here: have some rooms that could be let as lodgings, talk about the ozone in the air and the springs in the rocks."

They listened solemnly, and the innkeeper promised to paint out his " drapery " sign. I had four glasses of tea. I purchased two pounds of bread for my journey, and all this cost but fivepence. Still, if he had no more customers that day I supposed his takings would be up to the average. I am sure they had a lively topic of conversation for days to come about a real Englishman who had shown them the way to make the village a " going concern."

It was interesting to observe the impression made by the announcement that I was an Englishman. Englishmen are rather a myth in these parts. The wonders of London and New York must be taken on trust, without vouchers, like the miracles of the Bible, and I daresay that when one of us does turn up they take him as a sign which is not only sufficient guarantee for the reality of modern civilisation, but also for any points in their religion of which they may have doubt. It is, however, much more likely that they would doubt civilisation than the Bible, and they would accept the authenticity of Elijah's chariot sooner than that of flying machines.

CHAPTER XIX

"THROUGH SNOW AND ICE"

I TOOK the road to the Krestovy Pass. The clouds lowered, and there was the promise of much snow. It was bitterly cold, and the mountains in front were dressed from head to foot in white robes. Two versts from Kobi an avalanche had fallen recently, so that the road would have been impossible but for an emergency tunnel that had providently been constructed at that point. Fifty men were at work shovelling snow into the river-valley, which was itself piled up in bergs of snow. I wondered what was in store for me at the higher points of the road.

The snow came thick and fast, and the wind blew the tops of the drifts in my face. The snowy mountain sides seemed to faint as the clouds came over them. The river below me was absolutely hidden from view, but it rushed rapidly under the snow. They say the snow never completely melts from this river-bed, even in the hottest seasons.

I fastened my waterproof sleeping-sack about my person, for it was so cold. The road had now on each side of it an eight-foot wall of piled-up and drifted snow, and in this wall little snow caves had been dug out to allow the traveller or workman to take shelter in storms. I was among the elements, high up among the snowy peaks, with snow above and below. To the horizon ran curve after curve of undulating snow. Yet as I stood and listened I heard larks singing. There must be sheltered valleys somewhere.

Five miles from Kobi the road was completely closed to vehicular traffic by an immense heap of avalanche snow, fifty yards across. Over the chaos was a track fairly secure for pedestrians. Now and then one went up to the knee in loose snow. It was a grand pile which an English schoolboy would revel in.

I marvelled at the new world I had so suddenly entered. As the road grew higher all became whiter, till earth and sky were one and there was no dividing line. I felt among the clouds themselves. At Krestovy Pass there was no view to be seen—the hurrying storm closed in everything about my eyes. I looked downward into an abyss of snow and cloud. Then for a moment the storm seemed to be hurrying away from me. The snow ceased to fall on the road where I stood, but in front of me rushed in the gale. I saw the lines of distant precipices, and beyond, the peculiar greyness of the storm. Then the snow returned, and the wind was like to take one's ears off. The snow rushed past with extraordinary velocity. Often now the road was banked up fifteen feet with snow, so that one was in a sheltered passage. Coming once more into the open, I found the storm had slackened. A beam of the sun shot through, and showed behind the flakes tall, ghostly mountains with seams of awful blackness, where from their steep sides the snow had fallen away.

From the overtopping snow banks on the road hung icicles a yard long, and the walls of the dark emergency tunnels were sheeted with ice. In one of these near Gudaour the ice against the rock wall was fifteen feet high and three to eight feet thick. Huge icicles ten feet long hung from the roof. The tunnel was a fairy grotto. At the foot of the icicles were piles of little ice marbles where the frozen walls had thawed; the fanciful person might call them jewels. The whole was lovely to look at, for the outside surface of the ice was glittering lace-work.

I was now going lower and I noticed that it was milder—the snow was not so dry, and the roadway was wet and muddy. I witnessed an extraordinary phenomenon, the road steaming from the heat of the sun shining through the clouds, and yet the snow falling heavily all the time.

The descending road has a sheer precipice on one side, and the abyss might tempt the will of some people if they ventured near the edge. It was a strange sight to see the snowflakes being blown upward out of the valley of the River Aragva. I looked down three thousand feet and saw the pleasant green of the south

AKHTSAURI GLACIER, KAZBEK

country. I looked up to the north and saw the mountains cloaked and grim, like sentinels sitting at their posts.

Gudaour looked like the outskirts of Moscow in midwinter. The snow was piled up on each side of the road and on the cottage roofs. One would have said it was the month of January for certain.

I had two glasses of milk at one of the inns, and still felt in very good form for continuing on the road. It was an immediate descent, at first through slush of snow, and then over mud, and finally along a dry, hard highway. A thousand feet below the village it was raining; the weather was decidedly mild. At one spot it seemed to me I had located a type of English weather. But for the mountains it might have been a wet February day in Essex.

Then I found again wild snowdrops and violets, and the blackthorn was in bud. Two thousand feet below there were cowslips and lilies, and there, to my joy, the hot sun came out and clothed the spring in sparkles. I slipped down to Mleti and found the summer there.

CHAPTER XX

LAVRENTI CHAM KHOTADZE

"Thy form was plump, and a light did shine
In thy round and ruby face,
Which showed an outward visible sign
Of an inward spiritual grace."—PEACOCK.

MLETI stands on the White Aragva, a beautiful river of clear water, lifting thousands of white foaming ripples. A Russian poet has written:

"Day and night runs the Aragva unweariedly over the stones,
And golden fish dart under the sapphire waves."

The road goes through the valley of the Aragva for a distance of thirty miles through Pasanaour and Ananaour. I went on towards the first-named village, expecting to sleep there that night. But the unexpected happened. About two versts from Mleti I was sitting by the roadside when a priest came flying past me in a cart. He was shouting and singing, going downhill as fast as horse could carry him, and his long black hair streamed in the wind. Half-standing, half-sitting in the cart, he flourished a cudgel over the racing horse. When he saw me he made a movement to stop, but he was going too fast to pull up.

It was beginning to rain, and I promised myself to take shelter at the next inn along the road. I passed Arakhveti, a typical Georgian village, having an old church with a temporary tower of hay, and old hand-carved Ikons outside the door. There were a few cottages of the common type, having stone foundations and an upper storey of basket-work. A mile beyond this I came to a *Dukhan*, the first wine-house since Mleti. And there I saw the priest again.

He was sitting at a table outside the inn drinking wine with a party of Georgians. A pitcher was in the middle of the table and glasses all round. He hailed me and said he would willingly have driven me had he known in which direction I was going, and bade me sit down and drink wine. Asked from what province I came, I replied that I was English, which evidently made a great impression, though they immediately took the aspect of having met Englishmen every day of their lives. I subsequently learned that I was the first they had seen.

They spoke among themselves in the Georgian tongue, evidently discussing the democratic institutions of Great Britain, and then the priest said to me, " They keep us down, they don't educate us; they forbid us to have schools; they call us savages. What do you think of us Georgians—aren't we an unhappy nation? I myself am not an educated man. I finished the seminary, and then the Russian teacher said, ' Georgian, that is a dog's language,' and I gave up learning. But these," said he, pointing to his companions, "are as ignorant as the sheep, they know nothing. I proposed to build a school out of that old ruined barracks—it would have cost nothing; we ourselves could have built it, and I wrote a petition, but the Archbishop wrote back saying education wasn't necessary."

He bawled this speech at the top of his voice and shook his abundant black hair. His name, as I learnt afterwards, was Lavrenti Cham Khotadze; he was a handsome man, tall and strong, with red face and flashing eyes; his dense black eyebrows were too near together, so that when he was excited he looked mad. He had a fine long beard and a Roman nose. Over the wine cups he was certainly very uproarious, whatever he may have been in his church, and he emphasised his opinions by striking the table with his whole forearm. From head to foot he was enveloped in a dark blue cloak fastened with a belt at his middle.

A very dangerous political conversation ensued, and we drank a series of revolutionary toasts, one being that of the enemies of Russia—might they soon overcome her, and so let the Georgians gain possession of the Caucasus once more! They seemed to think that I might write to the English papers and fan up political animosity, and so help to bring about a European war, which would give the Tsar so much to do that the Caucasus would be enabled to gain its independence. They wished me to set the world on fire "to boil the Kaiser's eggs," as the saying is.

The rest of the party were well-dressed Georgians, but they did not enter into the conversation further than to confirm what the priest said. They were rather deficient in Russian. The priest himself a little discouraged the use of the Slavonic tongue, and made many malicious mistakes in his pronunciation when he used it himself. He constantly referred to the teacher who had called Georgian "*sobatchy yasik*"—dog's language—and he said to me, "Did God mean all people to be alike, I ask you?"

I replied that I thought not.

"You are not a Mahometan," asked one of the men; "you profess Jesus Christ; you are orthodox?"

I assented. "Orthodox" in Russia is as wide a term as "Christian."

"Well," said the priest, "God didn't intend us all to speak the same tongue or He would have given all the same sort of faces. Now, look at my face, you can't call *it* Russian."

One of the party pulled a grey hair from the pope's head, and there was much laughter. But one of the men said to me seriously:

"Don't think that we are irreverent; we are only joking, we are so happy to have met you."

This man was a carpenter and he put his personal case to me.

" Now, I am a carpenter," said he. " My father was a carpenter; we make no progress. Motor-cars come along the road. I don't understand them, but it is possible to understand them. If they taught me mechanics I could make them. Motor-cars weren't made by God, were they? They weren't even made by generals. Working men like myself made them. And haven't I got eyes, hands and brain as they? "

This was truly a beautiful utterance of its kind, and said with a touching simplicity that won the heart.

Uproarious Lavrenti rushed on:

" And the war against Japan which cost millions! What do you think of their making the Caucasians pay taxes? Why should we pay; did we order the war? Did we fight it? Let those who ordered pay. Now, if they'd sent me instead of old Kuropatkin, you'd have seen."

We drank a few more toasts and then it became time to go. There was one round more in the pitcher; the priest poured out a glass each and we all stood up whilst the last toast was proposed.

" The Mother of God save us! "

We drank it solemnly, but I heard one man add " some time or other." Whereupon the priest laughed whimsically.

Lavrenti asked me to accompany him in his cart

and sleep the night at his house. On the way he showed me his church—a chaste white chapel with a little green dome; it holds a hundred people, never more, and had been built in the ancient time when Rurik was Tsar of Russia. It has its own Georgian Ikons, though the Russians have taken out the precious stones.

His village was Nadiban. We did not get there before dark, but I heard the music of the guitar, and saw the youths and maidens of the village dancing the *lezginka*. I went into the poverty-stricken dwelling of the pope and saw his many little children. It was evident that his wife grumbled at him for bringing me home, and indeed there was no accommodation for visitors. The poor woman felt shamed. They made a bed up for me in a manger of the stable, and Lavrenti apologised, quoting that somewhat out-of-date proverb that " poverty is no sin," adding that Christ Himself had slept in a manger, and so perhaps I would not object. His wife sent in a pillow and a quilt. I wrapped myself up in my bed, and despite the snoring of a sheep with a cold, and the attempts of an ox to browse off my toes, I slept the sleep which is often denied to the just.

CHAPTER XXI

ON THE ROAD TO TIFLIS

I TOOK my leave of Lavrenti at dawn and set out for Pasanaour. A man with an ox-dray picked me up two miles from the priest's dwelling, and carried me ten miles at a pace slower than that of walking. The driver belonged to a tribe dwelling on the Black Aragva, consisting of about thirty thousand souls with a quite alien language and distinct customs, the *Khevsurs*. For one thing, they take their wives for a year on probation before marrying them. This man spoke no Russian, but a Georgian boy who was also being carried told me about him and his people. He pointed out how dirty he was, and showed a scar on his cheek and another on his wrist from knife wounds. The Khevsurs are a very quarrelsome tribe, and it is difficult to find a single grown man who has never been wounded. They live by shepherding and by wattle-making. Wattle is a very important manufacture in the Caucasus; houses and fences are made of it, and it is used for the embankments of the rivers.

The ox-cart left the road at the confluence of the Black Aragva with the White, and I was on my feet

GEORGIAN WOMEN

again. Many people were on the road, and these were more or less of a wilder type than those I had yet seen. I observed that when a man and woman make a journey together, the woman rides astride on horseback and the man walks at her side. The favourite colour for dresses seems to be a cloudy crimson.

I found the road monotonously beautiful. The hills were wooded to the top, the landscape was graceful. Here were more *pretty* things than on the north side of the Caucasus. One might have been in a park. Nature did not seem entirely responsible for the scene; a painter might have planned the grouping and effects; the country was, in a word, picturesque. The road seemed endlessly long, and I grew a little tired of it. The sun, however, was bright and hot, and I made a siesta among some rocks below the shelter of the road. There, in a cleft, beside the clear, rushing stream, I had a washing hour. It is wonderful how well one can wash and dry a garment or so in an hour. I dabbled the things in the water, and rubbed them and spread them in the sun to dry. Meanwhile a wren kept coming to and fro on tip-toe with thatch for a little house she was building under the bridge.

At the same time I also made a meal of bread and sausage helped down with water. Mountain bread is not good, but it has one advantage—it may be kept any length of time without its quality being obviously impaired.

Along the road are many extremely ancient ruins, and also buildings of great antiquity still inhabited. Clearly things last well in the Caucasian climate. The castles and towers are but toys compared with Norman ruins; they would have vanished utterly in England. The walls are so thin and so poorly put together. It seems that warfare has been rather more of a game than with us. There have been no Cromwells there. The churches, however, are often surrounded by high battlemented walls, which suggests that though there were no Puritans there were robbers in plenty.

Near Ananaour a flock of sheep, about a thousand, were driven past. One solemn shepherd marched in front of his flock, and at the sides young men scolded and yelled and kept the order with long poles. It was a grand sight. I came into the village, where there is an old Byzantine church with a castellated wall, and went into a tavern to get some bread and cheese and wine. Two men were at the table eating soup from one wooden basin with only a single wooden spoon between them. It was not really soup, but such a collection as no Western person could face—boiled maize, garlic, raw sliced onion, water and soaked bread. The two men eating were evidently chums, for instead of using the spoon each for himself, they helped one another, and I was specially amused to watch the little bald man near me shovelling the mixture into the mouth of his tall, hairy companion. As they were drinking yellow wine and I red, the little bald man proposed a health, and we changed glasses. Whereupon the company, for there were many present, viewed me with the utmost cordiality, and I shared among them the superfluity of my cold brown pitcher.

I set off towards Dushet, but feeling tired I spread my travelling-bed on a grassy bank and fell asleep. When I awoke it was dark and cold, and the sky was in continuous sheet lightning. A damp breeze blew briskly upon me and I was anything but comfortable. I lay for hours half-dozing, but at length came to the conclusion that it was better walking. Accordingly I continued my walk to Dushet. It was two in the morning, and even so early the sky promised dawn from three sides. I had no notion of the compass.

Very leisurely I made that walk. Ten miles is only a short distance at night, and I did not wish to arrive too early at Dushet. I promised myself hot tea, and I must not come too early for it.

It was a strange night, starless, dark, full of flower odours. I wished to drink, but every mountain stream was chalky. I sat on many stones and scanned the sky, hoping for the dawn. Dogs barked at me, and even made to attack me, but of human kind I saw none. I passed a beautiful dusky plum tree laden with blossom —she was a woman.

About half-past four I came into the district town of Dushet, and at five o'clock behold me sitting in an inn waiting for the samovar. " It will be ready at once, in an hour," the inn-keeper had said. On the wall of the inn was a large coloured picture of the Last Judgment, the good being led by angels to heaven, and the bad being clawed down into hell by fiends; it was very realistic, and caused me to recall the lines:

> " Hear all the pedants' screeds and strictures
> And don't believe in anything
> Which can't be told in coloured pictures."

The Georgians keep a good hot material hell in their conception of the hereafter.

The inn-keeper was evidently only just up, and didn't intend to serve customers before he had washed himself and put his shop in order. Accordingly, I watched his proceedings. He had a small wash, and combed his brown hair and moustache with two inches of comb, swept up the refuse from the floor, and put the empty bottles away. Large joints of mutton and beef hung from the roof—the man was also a butcher—and these he removed to a stall outside the shop. His wife slept in a bed in a gallery above the counter, and evidently slept too long, for her good man seemed to hurl imprecations at her from time to time.

At about half-past six the samovar, which had been " drawing " in the yard outside the shop, was brought in boiling, and I received what I had promised myself—four glasses of hot tea, the innkeeper's charge for which was ten copecks—twopence halfpenny.

I had no intention of walking this day. When I had finished my breakfast I went half a mile along the road and then sat down by the wayside. A quarter of an hour later a van carrying hay came along, and the driver offered to take me to Tiflis for a rouble. I lay down on two bags of chaff and soon fell fast asleep.

After about two hours I wakened up to find myself in heavenly circumstances; beautiful hills, a hot sun, a cool breeze and a comfortable resting-place. The driver also lay on two sacks and slept. The three horses clattered ahead, evidently well knowing the way.

So all day we rolled easily over the road as in a coach. The land was rich and beautiful, and the sun glorified every beauty.

At Mtskhet, the ancient capital of Georgia, we stayed for an hour, and I rested at a shop whose owners had gone to Tiflis for the day. Two little girls were in charge, and they gave me a dish of fish without knife or fork, and on protest brought out a carving knife! The elder girl was only twelve years old.

In the twilight we sped along the banks of the Kuma and arrived at Tiflis.

CHAPTER XXII

A TWO-HUNDRED-MILE WALK

I WAS at Kutais in the beginning of May, and I walked from that town two hundred miles across the Caucasus to Vladikavkaz, which I am told is a notable feat. It will certainly remain very notable in my mind, both in respect of the sights I saw and of the adventures I survived. I ascended from the Italian loveliness of Imeretia, where the wild fruit was already ripening in the forests, to the bleak and barren solitudes of Ossetia, where I had to plough my way through ten miles of waist-deep snow. I was attacked by roughs at Gurshevi and escaped from them only to lose myself on the Mamison Pass, where I found the road overswept by a twelve-feet drift of snow. I spent the night with shepherds on the pass in a koutan, a shelter for cows and sheep, half-house, half-cave, made of stones and mud. A shepherd showed me a track over the snow next morning, and after five hours of the most arduous walking I ever did in my life I reached the other side of the Caucasus. But I arrived there only to have a new adventure. A heavy snow-storm had come on so that it was difficult to find the road, and at Lisri I inquired of a hillman lounging in the way. This man arrested me as a spy and asked ten shillings to release me, and since I refused to pay the bribe I was hailed before the Ataman to give an account of myself. Such account proving unsatisfactory, I was formally arrested, and in fact remained a prisoner for five days. Strangely enough I was hospitably entertained during my captivity by chiefs and priests, but the fifth night I spent actually in prison, in a dirty Caucasian gaol with two robbers and a madman.

The air of Kutais is pungent with the fragrance of honeysuckle and sweet-briar, rhododendron and azalea—it tickles the nose. I set off on a peaceful Sunday morning when a sun hotter than we ever know in England, even in July, was flooding the valley of the River Rion with a superabundance of light and heat. The road, eighty miles long from Kutais to Oni, is perhaps the most beautiful in Europe, and this morning, its forested mountains bathed in grey-green loveliness and garlanded with flowers, it was a vision of Paradise. As a Georgian priest had said to me, " When you get there you will see; it is summer, everything is perfectly beautiful. It is heaven. If one were sent there after death one would not be disappointed."

I took it very easily this first beautiful day, and between dawn and sunset walked not more than twenty miles. The swallow-tail butterflies and large silver-washed fritillaries sipping honey from bush to bush probably strayed further than I did. I envied not at all the dozen people crammed into the Oni stage-coach—a vehicle constructed apparently out of currant boxes. In fact, the shorter distance traversed in a day the richer has been that day, one may say. The travellers on the stage-coach certainly didn't make a supper off wild strawberries as I did. That was the reward of my first day's sauntering. I found them that day. I did not find any more. The land became cooler and cooler, the next day and the next, till it was obvious I was travelling out of summer into winter again. But these strawberries were rich; they were nearly as large as thimbles, and I gathered about two pounds of them.

I slept that night under a rock a hundred feet above the road, and suffered no disturbance either from robbers or from bears. A soft rain plumped down just after sunset but I was in shelter. I slept, and indeed I could not say what happened that night beyond that the goddesses of sleep were gentle and kind to me. Just before dawn next morning I was awakened to hear the cuckoo calling from the dark forest opposite. Something in myself craved hot tea. I jumped up and took the road.

I swiftly walked the eight versts to Mekhven, where an innkeeper was taking down his shutters, and I persuaded the man to put up his samovar and give me tea. Tea is a luxury in these parts, for wine is the cheaper drink. It was no ordinary affair that a stranger should walk in at dawn and demand tea, and the innkeeper must have told at least ten villagers of the fact before he put a stick to the kettle. In five minutes his parlour was full of the curious. That I was English seemed to make a profound impression, but one man asked me whether our country was in the direction of Tiflis, and another whether it was nearer Persia or Japan. One thought Queen Victoria was on the throne; another asked if Russian was spoken in London, and were there many Georgians there. I had my tea, four glasses, and then drank the company's health in a tumbler of red wine. They replied, wishing me health on the road, and an affecting reception when at last I reached my hearth and home; might the English prosper and their king live long over them!—no doubt to the gratification of the shopkeeper, who filled a large pitcher from a half-deflated calf's skin under his counter. The population were of the sort " never deep in anything but wine."

The succeeding day was also one of full abundant sunshine. My roadside companions were large yellow rock roses and wild geraniums. In the woods I observed wild walnut trees and raspberry bushes. What feasts were promised for the later summer! I went forwards towards Alpani, meeting many Svani upon the road, a rather wilder tribe than usual, and very ignorant of the Russian language. With many of these I shook hands, however, that seeming to be the custom on the road. Five miles beyond Mekhven three Russian tramp labourers, of the type Gorky represented, wanted me to accompany them, but I declined. It was not easy to keep clear of them, however, and we kept meeting one another throughout the day. This was a day of thirst, as indeed might be said of many succeeding days. White wine and lemonade, red wine with radishes and bread and salt—no shop seemed to purvey more solid fare, and the only alternative to wine was water. But there is water on the road better than in the shops. I may safely say that if I have sampled all their wines I have also tried all their waters and tasted all the rock salts. There must be at least a score of varieties of water along the road, from streams like dilute quinine and iron to foaming seltzer water. In several villages the people fill a bucket with seltzer water every morning. Its taste is best just as it comes out of the rock. Near Alagir the River Ardon is white with sulphur, for there is an immense gushing sulphur spring there, and a natural manufacture of sulphurous and sulphuric acid. I suppose before ten years have passed someone will have found it advantageous to work this spring. The appalling smell of sulphuretted hydrogen should be sufficient advertisement. Indeed, the richness of the land from an industrial point of view, and its lack of development, is a fact which is bound to strike a modern European with wonder. Handsome copper and silver ore and delicious-looking asbestite are to be found with scarcely straying from the road.

At Zhouetti I stepped into an inn, and when the people heard I was an Englishman they sent across the way to a factory there and brought a German to see me, Herr Petersen, and we drank white wine and lemonade. He judged I must be hungry since one could get nothing fit to eat in these parts, and so ran back and fetched a box of sardines. So with unleavened bread and hard-boiled eggs I made a rough lunch there. At the factory is prepared barite powder, used in the manufacture of chintz. Herr Petersen was very kind, but counselled me against the natives.

I slept that night under a wall in a barley field and was very cold, so the next night I chose a better place, in the snug shelter of an overhanging rock, and screened from view by a full blooming hawthorn bush.

On the third day it rained much, and I spent some hours in caves or under trees. The verdure had a different aspect in the wet, and I reflected as I waited that the spring is not advanced by rain, but it gathers strength in the rain to proceed more quickly when the sun comes out. So with the tramp!

CHAPTER XXIII

CLIMBING INTO WINTER

THE Khvamli Table Mountain seems to stand as a fort between the north and the south, and it is an extraordinary sight. Its uppermost two thousand feet are naked of verdure. The grey cliff, a mile long, rises sheer from the crests of a green forest and extends in a regular battlemented array, which suggests a great city wall. On one side of that mountain I found summer, and on the other winter.

It was an extraordinary experience to climb out of an almost tropical summer into a land where the trees were only just budding, and the snowdrop and crocus were in bloom, and where the snow had not yet melted from the road. I had started on a Sunday when the weather approximated to that of July; on Friday I had reached March, and on Saturday I was in mid-winter.

I passed through Oni, an unusual town, in which scarcely a new house has been built since the twelfth century, and which is now inhabited by a tribe of mountain Jews living in peculiar isolation. This was on Thursday afternoon, and I spent the night in an inn nine miles north, at the little town of Utsera, now fast becoming a popular health resort though a hundred miles from a railway station. It is about the height of Mount Snowdon, on the fringe of an ancient pine forest. At Utsera it was raining on the Friday morning. At the next village, Glola, a thousand feet higher, the rain was changed for sleet. The road ascends through a fir wood said to be the grandest in the Caucasus; the pines are as broad-trunked as some of our famous oaks, and they rise straight as a die to almost incredible height. Their ancient hoariness and greyness add to their majestic appearance.

I was now nearing the neck of the mountains and stormy Mamison. The Rion, broad at Kutais, was here but a small torrent. The road, if such it can be called, was traversed by many cascades and broken away by rocks and rivers, so that a horseman could pass only with difficulty. To vehicular traffic it was completely closed. Sitting at any point of the road one could count literally scores of uprooted pines. Above Glola the sun came out, the same hot Caucasian sun, though tempered by the cold air, and, as if to pretend that summer was there, the Camberwell Beauty butterfly (of name obviously not universal) flitted to and fro flaunting its purple and gold. Under the pine trees were wild snowdrops thick clustered, and on the roadway even little purple crocuses.

The road became difficult to manage, two bridges

having been entirely washed away. I had at one point to leap fifteen feet on to a black snowdrift, which I feared might give under me. But I succeeded and won my way to Gurshevi. That was the first village of the Ossetines, and had generally a bad name. Some years ago an explorer and two guides disappeared entirely in this region, and have never been heard of since. And I had an adventure there which greatly alarmed me. I had not stopped at the village; it was difficult of access, being upon a cliff, and I strode forward toward the pass. But a verst forward on the road I was hailed from a distance by four roughs, who demanded a rouble. I hurried on. They called " Stop! " But I paid no attention, seeing that they were extremely heavily clad and could not hope to catch me up; they were in a valley about five hundred feet below. The road, however, was extraordinarily tortuous, and if I had only climbed straight up the cliff to the pass I should have saved myself at least five miles walking, and my encounter with the roughs into the bargain. They were able to cut me off and get into hiding among the boulders and rocks above the road. My position was sufficiently dangerous, but I did not guess their intention; they had no guns. Fortunately I caught sight of one of them running from one rock to another, and when I came to the district I stopped short and demanded of my hidden enemies what they wanted. For answer a large lump of rock came whizzing through the air within two inches of my head. Had I been struck I should have been stunned. Whilst I was deliberating a second followed, almost more terrifying than the first, and coming with great force, being hurled from above. No one was to be seen. There was but one thing to do. I lifted up my legs and sprinted.

I did not cease running till I was well up the pass and in a region where there were no loose rocks to be found. The snowy peaks had now become unveiled, and the fir forest was left behind. I thought that if I hurried I might get over the pass that day. My assailants were far behind. I did not fear another ambush. What was my surprise, however, to see suddenly in front of me two men walking towards me. Their dog rushed at me. I received him with equanimity, being much more afraid of men than of beasts. They told me there was no road for ten versts and would not be for a month, and they advised me to go back to Gurshevi. I listened with trepidation and could not believe what they said. I agreed to their advice, however, but said I would rest a little as I was very tired, and bade them go on in front. When they were out of sight I left the road abruptly and struck straight up the turfy bank towards the pass. I crossed the circuitous road three times and came to the region of continuous unmelted snow. I dragged myself through a mile of " slosh," where a profusion of yellow water-lilies were growing, and for the best part of an hour I strove to find the road again. When I found it and followed it I came rapidly to snow too soft and deep to pass; indeed, twenty yards in front the road was perfectly lost in the snow, unmarked by undulation or rift in the even whiteness.

I was desperate, but I felt sure there was a way, for I had heard of hillmen coming from Utsera, and had been even counselled to wait for a companion there. I resolved to get a shepherd to show me the way, and with that in view climbed awkwardly downhill to the turfy region, where a flock was browsing. Yes, there was a way—one quite different from the road; an Ossetine shepherd offered to show me for a shilling. I agreed on condition that he first gave me a glass of milk, for I was exhausted and had eaten nothing since morning. This man was friendly enough, but on consideration he thought it impossible to show me that night. I should have to wait until next morning. I might sleep with them in their koutan if I didn't mind the filth; they would make a bonfire and a big supper. His mate, Gudaev, would play the fiddle; I could sing. He would roast two quails which Achmet had killed; they would all have a jolly evening, and to-morrow morning very early he would take me and show me the track. Very thankfully I agreed.

CHAPTER XXIV

A NIGHT IN A KOUTAN

CHEKAI and his companion shepherds living in the koutan were clad in rags that were extremely dirty, their faces red, unshaven and wild, and their feet and legs bare, except of dirt. They were extremely apologetic. "You are clean," said Gudaev, "but God has given us to work in filth, as you see, but we are men and Christian Ossetines." I put them at their ease with a smile and went to inspect the koutan. It was an extensive dwelling, for the most part dug out of the mountain side. The walls were made of boulders plastered wind-tight with stable filth, the roof of pine branches, peat and hay. There were no windows, and so the whole had no light beyond what came in at the door, or from the hole in the roof; but what light there was sufficed to show that the house was divided by fences into a number of compartments for the reception of horses, cows, sheep and goats.

One of these compartments, in the shelter of a ponderous rock, was the shepherds' own room. Three bits of fir trunk made the seats, and between these trunks and the walls were the beds of hay where they slept. Under the rock the red-grey embers of last night's fire still smouldered. I went in and sat down, being tired and cold after my wanderings in the wet snow on the pass. Chekai and his companions milked the cows, brought in the horses and the sheep, separated and drove into separate pens the rams, the ewes and the lambs, so that the dark koutan became full of the cries of animals. I myself assisted in the separating of the sheep, for Chekai, who had asked my name, kept calling out, " Stepan, come here," " Stepan, go there," and I was fain to obey.

Achmet brought me the two quails he had killed, and showed me them with pride. He must have been a sure marksman with stones, and I thought with some ruefulness of my recent encounter when I had been somewhat in the position of the poor quails, but I said nothing. Gudaev, having milked the cows, took up the business of hacking firewood out of a tough pine log. In his intervals of rest he brought armfuls of wet branches and put them on the fire. I was given a wooden basinful of fresh milk, which Achmet had strained through hay before giving me. Presently the animals were all housed and a bonfire made up on the rude hearth. Clouds had crawled once again into the evening sky, there was a flash of lightning and a long roll of thunder; the dancing hailstones rushed down, and following them thick, soft, flaky snow.

A KOUTAN

I was glad I had not tried to cross the pass that night.

It was very dark, and the wet wood was filling the koutan with smoke, but Chekai, who had cut up a great number of little sticks, made a brilliant illumination by setting fire to them. They had a contrivance of tin about three feet from the ground, and in this they burned the resinous pine splinters for hours. At length the brushwood burst into flame and dried and caught the thicker branches; in half an hour we had a roaring big fire. Gudaev hung a large iron pot over it and boiled water; Chekai settled down to pluck the quails; Achmet prepared to make bread. When the water had boiled Chekai informed me they would make copatchka. Achmet took maize flour, salt and milk and boiling water, and kneaded a dough into flat cakes about the size of soup plates. Gudaev stood them on end in front of the fire, and toasted them first one side and then the other. When they were done he buried them under the grey-red ashes and left them to cook. This done, he took from a wooden peg in the mud of the wall an iron violin with two strings, and commenced a tune of that sighing and moaning and shrieking style characteristic of Caucasian music. Chekai sang, and all the while plucked the little quails. When the birds had been quite disfeathered, singed and cleaned, the shepherd transfixed them together on a stake and toasted them at the fire. Achmet filled up the pot over the fire with milk, flour and salt, thereby preparing soup.

I had fallen back asleep when suddenly Chekai called out, " Stepan, get up and eat! " This I was not loth to do, and in a minute behold me tasting for the first time hot copatchka and roast quail. It must be said the bird was tasty though it was small. The milk soup made my teeth dance, it was so hot. Chekai began a conversation. " What are the English—Christians or Mahometans? " asked he. " Is England far away? Where does it lie? " I replied that it was four or five thousand versts to the north-west. Chekai whistled. " Beyond the mountains? " said he. " And have they such poor and dirty people there? Look how poor I am, look how I'm dressed."

" I expect you're not so poor as you look," said I. " The owners of the sheep must pay you well, but you leave the money in the village with your wife and family, or your mother."

The shepherd frowned and then grinned. I had apparently hit on the truth.

The time came to make an end of the feast and lie down to sleep. They gave me the best place between a fir plank and a sheep fence close to the hot embers. I covered myself entirely up in my travelling-bed, and was secure in that both from vermin and from dirt. The three others disposed themselves in different parts of the smoky cavern and began to snore horribly. I slept heavily.

At dawn, through custom, I awoke. Chekai was already stirring and had gathered fresh wood for the fire. He warned me it was necessary to hurry if he was to show me the track, for he had much work to do. I showed immediate alacrity. The weather seemed promising, and I was full of hope that I should reach the other side of the mountains in time for breakfast. We had a ten minutes' parley over money. Chekai wasn't quite sure that he couldn't hold me up to ransom *à la Hadgi Stavros*. But he was eventually content to receive half-a-crown, together with the present of a pretty water-jar I had bought a week before in Georgia, and which he coveted. In exchange for the water-jar he presented me with his staff, which was stout and long and served me better in the long run than I could have guessed. I ought to have taken another meal of copatchka and milk before starting. A bottle of vodka in my pocket would not have been amiss. I did not dream that after two hours' walking my heart would be beating so violently through exertion that I should fear to perish in the snow.

CHAPTER XXV

OVER MAMISON

I FOLLOWED my guide Chekai over the mountain marsh, where hundreds of bright yellow water-lilies were in blossom. The sun had just risen, the clouds were very white, and the clear sky was lambent greenish blue. " It's going to be fine," said the shepherd. " You'll get across safely. In an hour you will come to the Southern Shelter, a white house; you can go in there and rest, and one of the soldiers will show you the way on. After the pass there is another house, but if it is stormy you won't be able to see it for the snow. Never mind, you will hear the bell. There are two men on duty night and day, and they are obliged to ring the big bell whenever it is stormy. Perhaps they don't ring it now in the winter, I don't know; I've never been over before June when the road is black. Not more than four Ossetines have been over this month, but the soldiers go backwards and forwards seven or eight at a time.

We came to the margin of the unmelted snow and followed a track for about a mile, and then my companion began to complain that his feet were getting frozen, and I told him that if I was now on the right track I could dispense with him; he might go back. This evidently he was glad to do. I paid him a rouble in small change, every coin of which he said was bad, and we had to test them separately on a bit of rock before he would be satisfied. We then exchanged presents, blessed one another and parted.

I was walking on a white carpet apparently boundless. To right and to left and ahead the rocks lifted themselves aloft in white masses. In the sky the clouds, torn as by storm winds, rushed hither and thither, now veiling the peaks and now the road, or filtering upward and downward at the neck of the pass. Here is the place where the weather is manufactured and shared out between north and south. The sky promised everything on the shipman's card. The sun suddenly shone out and flashed over all the snow with blinding brilliance, and then almost as suddenly became overcast as a foaming wave of cloud was tossed over it. I began to fear that the mists might hinder my crossing, or keep me waiting for hours on the desert of snow, afraid to go forward.

The ascent became more arduous. The snow was softer, and the surface not frozen hard enough to bear me. At every third step I sank to the knee; the staff the shepherd had given me saved me once or twice, but I could never tell when I should be upborne by the snow and when I should sink. After half a mile of this I stopped and gasped. I thought I couldn't get on. Storm, however, threatened. I must go on. I took another step and sank as deep as it is possible for one leg to go. In pulling myself out I fell on one shoulder and almost went out of sight. It was like the hindered progress in a nightmare. I must have rested ten minutes before I set forward again, and walked fifty yards by three steps and a fall irregularly along the faint track. I felt like Dorando at the finish of his race at Earl's Court.

An hour's struggle brought me to the Southern Shelter, a military station cold and uninviting, but even so a delight to my eyes, a very oasis in the wilderness. I saw no one there, and therefore did not stop. It seemed to me I must soon reach the summit. I was, however, destined to disappointment. The track now led up a steep bank, a weary way. I was constantly up to the waist in snow, and not a step that I took seemed to grip or take me appreciably forward. To add to the difficulties, the snow of last night's storm had almost completely effaced the track; it was only with the greatest difficulty that the eye discerned and traced the way. One false step and I should have gone slithering over the snow into the abyss like a riderless sledge. The clouds above my head massed and the snow-flakes hurried down. I sat down on my travelling-bed and surveyed the grim, silent snowstorm; to me it was then a dreadful sight, and I began to ask myself if this would not perhaps turn out to be my last upon this bright world. A flash of lightning and the long roll of thunder quickened my fears. I started up again and battled forward. It was an almost heart-breaking business truly. Every ten yards I came to a standstill with heart palpitations, caused partly, perhaps, by the rarity of the atmosphere—I suppose at nine thousand feet the atmosphere is rarer—but caused in most part, without doubt, by my exertions; and my sunburnt hands had become violet in colour. All about me the storm raged and the mist hid the crest of the pass.

The thunder rolled once more, and then unexpectedly the sun shone through the snow-flakes. The veiled mountains looked like workmen disturbed while up to their eyes in some job. I looked along my way to the crest of the mountain. It seemed to lead right up into the sky. It would have been an ideal road for the poet Davidson. I whispered to myself his lines:

"Alone I climb
The rugged path that leads me out of Time."

Then, after what seemed ages of slow dying, I saw in front of me the cross which marks the highest point of the pass. I did the impossible; I reached that cross. The reader may imagine the bliss I experienced sitting on my waterproof at its foot. Even if I perished in the descent I had now been a victor; henceforth there were no more Alps.

Downward was not so difficult. I even ran as if on

skis till I realised the danger of breaking my legs. It was a delightful contrast, however, the slipping downhill, the falling, jumping, plunging downward. My heart was light.

I had not descended five hundred feet before I saw an extraordinary sight—a hanging, frozen avalanche waiting for the snow, a long, high wall of fixed but sliding snow frozen and glittering, myriadfold icicled, and not white but pale green. Seen from below the long pale-green wall looked ominous beyond words. A new danger now presented itself to my mind—that of being swept away by falling snow—and suddenly this was emphasised. I heard a long, low, sullen roar that could not be thunder, but which I could not locate. It was followed by a second which seemed an echo, and by a third. Then, looking to a peak, I saw the cause of one, a falling drift of snow. I saw the slow-moving white descending, descending, and then suddenly splashing over the cliff in brown mud. Fast after and before followed the stones. The danger from falling drifts was imminent, and I kept my eyes open. The storm cleared. The bell was not ringing at the bell-house, and I did not stay there. On my way down I met a man toiling upward, and I felt exceedingly overjoyed, and thought to talk with him, but he was pale as a ghost and utterly exhausted. Beyond greeting, and an inquiry as to the state of the road, I got no further word from him.

In half an hour I was out of the snow on to the black road, and presently I came to the first village on the north side. The inhabitants all gathered round me and stared, and asked where I had come from and congratulated me. One old man in particular shook hands with me, effusively calling me *molodetse*, " fine fellow," and everyone seemed to combine to smile upon me. I was happy. One thing, however, was wanting—food. The village could only supply me with cold copatchka and salt.

CHAPTER XXVI

ARRESTED

I HAD been tramping almost three weeks when I crossed the snow of Mamison. I was therefore full of longing for the comforts of the town and calculated that in three days I should clear the remaining hundred miles and be resting in snug quarters. I was, in fact, full of such thoughts as I reached the village of Lisri, but, as Leonid Andrief says, " Man shall never know the next step for which he raises his tender foot." At Lisri I was arrested.

The village is a straggling one, built out of grey stone and put together from the remains of ancient ruins. In the barrenest of pasture land, and having no more than three months' summer, it is strange that anyone should have chosen to live there. Yet there is a large population of Ossetines. What they do beyond shooting bears and wild oxen by day and listening to the wolves at night it would be difficult to say. This day, however, there was unusual animation in the place. The priest had summoned all his parishioners and laid before them a proposal to build a new church and enlarge the school. It was a festive occasion, and probably more spirits were drunk that was conducive to my safety. In Ossetia there is little wine, but all the natives drink *Araka,* a home-brewed spirit suggesting gin in appearance but possessing the odour of stale whisky. It is made from fermented maize.

The man who arrested me was a primed villain. He reported me to the Ataman as a spy, and said I pretended to be ignorant of the Georgian language, but that he had trapped me into using some words of that tongue. He did not say he had offered to release me for ten shillings, and that he had proposed to discuss the bargain at a lonely point of the road two miles outside the village, and wished to accompany me thither. I had a very likely fear that he would have cut my throat and pushed me over the cliff into the snowy Ardon valley. He reminded me forcibly of some words a Russian had said to me: " The Ossetines have a tariff now—to lay a man out, one rouble; to murder him, three roubles."

I argued, coaxed, threatened, bluffed, all without avail: my captor was merciless. I must say I mistrusted him dreadfully, and I would not have paid the bribe had I had the money ten times over. I went back to the village and he followed me. I tried to inveigle him into conversation with a group of villagers. I appealed to them and told my story in Russian; they favoured me, and told the fellow to let me go. With their moral support I attempted an escape, and I should have got clear away, but for the fact that at that moment a party of horsemen were coming down into the village and I was cut off by them. My captor was not angry; his only concern was to get me by myself. My care was to start a big dispute with each newcomer. At length I demanded to be taken to the Ataman, and in this I was successful. The man who arrested me wanted me to come home with him, but I outwitted him.

I was brought to the village schoolroom, where the priest was holding his meeting. Fifty men seemed to be all shouting at once. The business in hand was interesting; the clergyman had called them together to do work, provide material and offer money for the construction of the new buildings, and also to discuss the plans. A church in an Ossetine valley costs little; it is made of stone and pine without windows or seats; the whole village is idle and ready to build a house of God for themselves just as they would build a new cottage. The question of wages is not heard. Ruskin himself could not have wished for a more complete absence of the principles of the " dismal science."

From the moment I entered I saw that the priest would be my friend. I was feeling desperately tired after climbing Mamison. I had used all my wits to get clear of the Ossetine, and now I fell back in exhaustion. I answered or failed to answer the questions of the inquisitive for hours. The Ataman came and questioned me lazily; in his heart he cursed his lieutenant for arresting me. He said to the people, in the Ossetine language, that if I escaped none was to hinder me. Several signalled to me to bolt, for everyone looked very kindly. But my captor hung on; there was no escaping him. He got me alone again, and tried to bully me with words into paying him the ten shillings. This was in the now empty schoolroom. I insisted on marching up and down, for it was cold, and for a quarter of an hour I listened to the man swearing at me.

Then the priest sent for me, and I was glad to get into better company. He was still surrounded by a crowd of villagers, but he saved me from my captor, taking me by a side door, and handing me over to his womenfolk to feed. I felt the brotherhood of educated men all over the world as he said to me *sotto voce*, " I am sorry to see you, a cultured man, in such a plight." His wife was very kind to me and brought me minced mutton and scones and araka and tea. I felt myself in a quiet haven out of the storm.

My captor made two further attempts to gain possession of me, and even succeeded once, under pretext of taking me to the Ataman. But when I found I was being taken to his home I refused to move a step, and seeing the priest in the distance I shouted to him and ran towards him. The upshot of a long dispute was that the priest overruled the fellow and took me to his own house for the night. I returned, and Khariton, for such was his name, accompanied me. We had a new meal, and my host put off his priestly garments and made merry. He and his wife were a very young couple who were very fond of one another, and played practical jokes of an elementary order, such as pulling one another's hair—the priest's hair being almost as long as his wife's.

Of the impressions of a very pleasant, convivial evening, what will chiefly remain in my memory is the discovery by Khariton of a small geography book, from which he read in a loud voice all that was said both in large print and in small about England. England had at last become for them an actually existent country. The good man had, however, seen an Englishman before. Some years ago one came up the valley prospecting for minerals. He could not speak a word of Russian, and he sat so funnily on his horse that all the natives laughed.

Did I know Professor Müller—professor of Asiatic languages at St Petersburg? He was a man to know. He came to Lisri some years back, and conversed with the natives in their own language so perfectly that they thought he must be an Ossetine.

Poor Khariton! he did not really know much of education. He confessed to me he was ready to die of shame when he had to speak with an educated Russian. But the Ossetines had few chances. It would be better later. They had schools and were learning. He was

AN OSSETINE DWELLING

teaching the village what he knew, little though that were. They had, moreover, arranged for the improvements—on the morrow all that had been volunteered would be written down.

I asked him what would happen to me. He thought I should be released. Had he been in my place he should have died of fright, he said. But I might be easy in my mind. The Ataman had received a circular from the Governors, and he did not understand its meaning. He would probably send me to the next village, to the Ataman of Zaramag. The latter was an educated man and would see that a mistake had been made.

At ten o'clock Khariton and his wife spread a bed for me on the floor and I was glad to lie down. So, with slumber closing weary eyes, ended for me this distressing and adventurous day.

CHAPTER XXVII

FIVE DAYS UNDER ARREST

NEXT morning I was sent under escort to the village of Zaramag, ten miles distant. But before starting Priest Khariton said to me, " I see that you have some of our copatchka in your satchel; permit me to give it to our dog, my wife will give you something fit to eat." And the kind woman filled my bag with scones and cake and eggs.

I was sent in charge of a very old man to the Ataman of Zaramag. I might easily have escaped, but it seemed more interesting to remain a prisoner. Outside Lisri he showed me a pool of human blood on the road where there had been a fight the night before. They are evidently rather rough in this district. I felt rather safer as a prisoner than if I had been at liberty.

We passed several small villages, one of which was Tli, an accumulation of broken-down towers; twelfth-century ruins patched together for the housing of the people of to-day. We were stopped here; someone called to us from the cliff. " There is a man dead," said my escort. " We must go up here." We climbed up accordingly, and found all the men of the village collected together, sitting on pine logs. Two men came rapidly forward to greet us, and we stood as it were on a threshold, while these proclaimed something in a loud voice in the Ossetine language. I think it meant, " In the name of the Father, the Son and the Holy Ghost. Amen," or the equivalent of that. We took off our hats and crossed ourselves, I following the example of my companion. With that someone took our things from us and put them aside, and we entered into the assembly and took seats on the logs. Everyone had goats' horns, from which they were drinking, and a vessel of that kind was brought to me full of *araka*, and with it hard-baked millet cake and salt. Everyone seemed to be serious, and to judge by the activity of three men going to and fro with copper kettles replenishing the horns, all were drinking hard. He who had died had been a very poor old man, but if he had been twice as poor and twice as miserable in his life I am sure his death would have none the less proved an excuse for the glass.

The Ataman of Zaramag was present, and my guard gave him the letter, in which he was asked if he knew anything against me, or who I was. He said the letter was unintelligible to him, and that I should have to be sent back, but all the same he sent me on to Zaramag to wait for him.

I waited there all day with a drunken Russian clerk

who wanted to borrow money to buy a quart of *araka* in order to drink my health. His wife, however, to save him the disgrace, now produced a bottle which she had previously hidden from him, and he proceeded once more to add water to the ocean.

It was yet early in the morning, but I spent the rest of the day with the man and his wife, drinking tea and listening to the confused boastings and witticisms of the drunkard. The Ataman remained at the burial-feast.

In the afternoon I grew tired of waiting and said I would walk on to the next village, and that if the Ataman wanted me he could send for me, and I strolled out accordingly. The clerk seemed paralysed by faith, and just sat and stared in amazement. I walked out of the village and took the road. There, however, I met the Ataman, who smiled amiably and re-conducted me to the abode of the clerk.

I spent that night in an almost sumptuous apartment in the house of the Ataman. First he entertained me at dinner, and we ate mutton and drank sweet Ossetinsky beer from a wooden loving-cup. Obviously being arrested has its advantages.

The next day I was sent to the Ataman of Nuzal, asking what he had to say about me. For some time I had thought I should have been returned to Lisri, but the drunken clerk had intervened and advised that I be sent further. The boy who should have taken me went without me, however, and I was put into the charge of a carter going that way.

The road now led downhill, and I left the snow behind. The valley of Zaramag, which might be called a nursery of rivers, has a wild beauty, though it came harshly upon my eyes after the soft luxuriance of the South. We followed the river Ardon through the wonderful gorge of Kassar. The little thread of road runs unobtrusively through ten miles of ruined cliffs. Far below the little river agonises, roars and conquers. The height, the depth, the gloom, the chaos of decay and ruin—these appal the vision. It is more dreadful and uninhabitable than the gorge of Dariel, a dangerous district, moreover, where man needs fear the bear and the wolf. Above a glacier my guide pointed out to me specks which he said were bison.

We arrived at Nuzal in the afternoon and there a comedy enacted itself. The Ataman refused to receive me or to have anything to do with me, declaring he had no authority to arrest me. "What shall I do?" asked the carter. "That's nothing to do with me," answered the Ataman. "Do you hear?" said the carter to me. "The Ataman won't take you; go and beg him to take you, or else you'll have to go back to Lisri."

"I shan't go a single step back upon the road," said I.

"You will be forced," said he.

"Then I shall be forced," I replied. "They'll have to carry me."

"But what shall I do?" asked the carter. "I'm going to Ardon on business. I can't take you back."

No one would have anything to do with the poor man. A Russian visiting doctor came up and talked to me, and when he heard of the dilemma he was like to die of laughter. The idea that the Ataman of a remote village should have arrested a European tourist tickled him immensely. He promised to write my story in the Russian newspapers. "Let him go," said he; "and as for that," pointing to the letter, "throw it away."

"I must have a receipt," said the carter.

"I'll give you one," said I.

The upshot was, however, that I agreed to go a stage further, to Misure, where there is a silver factory and a telephone to Vladikavkaz. It was a Belgian factory, and M. Devet was a very nice man. I agreed to that, but at Misure the telephone was out of order, and beyond drinking a bottle of wine between us we gained no comfort there. I counted myself free really, for certainly the carter was without authority, but it was interesting to see what would happen next, and I forebore to escape. The man cursed his stars for having taken me, but he was obsessed by a sense of duty. He would take me on to Alagir and hand me over to the Pristav there. To Alagir we went accordingly. *En route,* however, we slept in a little shop by the wayside, and it was not till next morning that we passed through the gorge of Ardon with its hot sulphur springs, and came to the large settlement on the steppes known as Alagir.

At the Pristav's office we had to wait five hours, and I was assured I should be liberated, but then I found they dared not release me. I had to go to Ardon, fifteen miles distant.

As I was leaving Alagir there was a strange incident. A well-dressed man, whom I mistook for a member of the Russian Secret Police, came up to me, and tried to get me to say things against the Russian Government and my treatment. "You can speak to me as to a mate," said he. "I also am a *politikan.* What happened to you? You are exhausted. Never mind. Bear up." He spoke a few words aside to my guard, and then went on again. "I have arranged," said he. "You won't go just yet. You must come along with me and have a meal, then I will take both of you in a cart, and we can have a chat." I felt suspicious and refused.

Meanwhile two young men came up and entered into conversation with him, and they asked me my story. I told them, and one said, "We represent the Society for the help of educated Ossetines in distress; we beg you to receive our help." Then one gave me five separate ten-copeck pieces and a slip of paper with his address, saying, " If you are in difficulty write to me. You will need money before you are released—to this little you are welcome."

Again I refused and thanked them profusely. Then the first man said he must have offended me. I insisted that he hadn't, and we parted. I have every reason to believe that they were very honest and good people, though their manner was not very assuring. My guard, who had patiently waited, now went on and I followed.

From Ardon I was sent to a place called Ard-Garon, where I spent the night at the house of a hospitable Ossetine. I arrived in the evening, and my host took me out for a walk on the steppes to what he called a " mayovka," so called because it was held in the month of May. It was an evening picnic of about fifty Ossetine men. There were no women. They had buckets of *araka* and baskets of mutton and bread. I politely partook of their viands.

From Ard-Garon I was exported to Gizel, where my good fortune seemed to suffer eclipse. I was thrust, in spite of my protests, into the village gaol, there to exist from three in the afternoon till eight next morning. I had had nothing to eat all day and nothing was obtainable here. Only, in answer to my complaint, the gaoler put in a pail of dirty water that I might drink if I wanted to.

At Ardon an official had said to me, " We can't

keep you here because we've nowhere to put you. You wouldn't like to lie in prison, would you? Have they prisons in England? . . . Clean ones, I suppose. But ours are dirty. Would you like to see ours? " He burst into a guffaw of laughter. But the Ataman said to him, " No, no, you needn't go out of your way to do that."

I suppose the place was ugly. I did not guess that on the succeeding night I should be for the first time in a Russian gaol.

It was a verminous cell, with holes in the rotten flooring and no glass in the barred windows. The door was cased in iron; the walls hung in tatters of broken plaster. There were no seats, but at one end some planks served for a bed. My companions were an Ossetine and an Ingoosh, both charged with stealing, and a madman, who was, I understood, a regular tenant of the den. I had obviously nothing to do with these people and didn't belong to their class. They were as selfish as possible, and I suppose I should have had a bad night but for the fact that I was so worn out. I huddled myself together on the planks and slept. At Vladikavkaz next day, the Chief of Police inspected my passport, and bade me take my liberty and " live with God."

CHAPTER XXVIII

MR ADAM

TRAMPS often bring blessings to men. They are very brotherly; they have given up the causes of quarrels. Perhaps sometimes they are a little divine. God's grace comes down upon them.

Certainly one day I met a noble tramp, an Eden tramp. He came upon me at dawn with a wood smile on his old face. He was one of the society of tramps; he knew all Russia, its places and peoples, and he called himself Mr Adam. Why did he adopt that name—why had he thrown away the other name? These were questions he was not in a hurry to answer. They involved a story. Such a story! It sounded in my ears like a secret melody of the world. But first let me say how I met this most jovial wayfarer.

I had slept one night by the side of the road among nettles and thistles. My pillow was a stone, my bed soft, dusty earth. I was so near to the road that the lumbersome, creaking ox-carts, that approached and passed in the night, seemed within arm's reach—so near that I felt the movement in the air as they passed.

Horses snorted uneasily now and then, and once in the early morning a dog came snuffing among the herbage after me. It was a night of dew and dust. I do not suppose I slept more than three hours, but it did not seem a long night. The approach of dawn came as a surprise to me. I was glad to think it was dawn even if it should turn out to be an illusion. My bed was too cold and fresh, my eyes seemed clammy and sticky, as if spun together with gossamer threads, my forehead was heavy as iron, my body seemed long and ponderous as that of a trold. Everything in me waited for the sun. A night on the mountains gives its peculiar refreshment; it nurses each limb in cold, dewy air, and transmits its influence in cold thrills into the very depths of one.

I sat up and surveyed the scene in the half light, and what was my surprise to see an apparently monstrous figure of a man coming toward me along the road. I almost feared him, but I soon saw his peculiar smile of geniality and my fears gave way. This was Mr Adam. He came up to me as if he had known me from the cradle. The usual greeting and question passed, and then he pulled out of his ragged overcoat a chunk of bread and some hard white cheese, and sat down on a stone with the evident intention of breakfasting. I bade him wait whilst I filled my kettle. Whilst I went to get water he lit a fire. We had a very cheery meal. He cut his bread and cheese with a rusty dagger!

He told me how he came to take the name of

Adam, in memory of an old companion of the road who made a poor woman in Vladikavkaz very happy. This is the story. There was a man named Peter who died, leaving a widow and three children. The woman was very young and had a baby at her breast and was without money. When she had paid for priest and coffin there was little left her. Her husband had been a writer in a railway office; he wrote envelopes and copied letters. He only received forty roubles a month and was very improvident. Though perhaps it was not he, but Society, that was improvident; for his wife was a good woman and her children worthy. And when one is young one does not expect to die.

Anna, for such was her name, had to leave the house where Peter had died. She had to step down in the world. She took one room in a little cottage, and lived there, and waited to starve. Neighbours helped her, but they were very poor, and her babes, like young birds in the nest, all stretched out their mouths to her and cried.

It was a bare room. The family slept upon the floor. There was an old table that had been lent to them, and a stool and a box. In a corner the Ikon picture gleamed. The woman was little clothed, and the children showed their little white bodies. So much had been sold to get a little money for food that even the samovar was not seen. Neighbours coming in held up their hands in pity of their poverty.

But their fortune changed a little, for one day a strange chance befell. Anna had made a fire between some stones in the yard of the cottage, and was cooking a mixture in a pot when a ragged old man came up and begged a taste of the soup. She looked at him and thought how strange it was that anyone should beg of her, and then she refused him, saying, " I am as poor as you, good man, and my soup is bad, for it is what I have myself gathered. I took my pot to the market and begged. It is the first time, and it feels very strange. Everyone knew I did not beg for money, only for food. Some put in fruit, and some poured in milk; others threw in biscuits; near the butchers' line I got a piece of meat, and by the vegetable stalls I picked up some cabbage leaves and an old cucumber. It is very well. I shall go every morning and we shall not starve. Only the soup is for us and it will not be good for others."

The old man was tall and very hairy; one could scarcely see his face for hair, and through the rents of his ragged red shirt one saw his brown hairy chest. His overcoat was of many colours and many cloths; he had evidently sewn into it whatever cloth he had picked up during many wanderings, and he had lain in it in many muds and soils, and the stains remained. His legs were tied up in sacking like trees protected from the winter, and his boots, which he had made himself without leather, were little bags of wool and shavings and grasses and dandelion down. He was not, however, the least self-ashamed.

He did not reply to Anna's refusal for some minutes, but he stood watching, fumbling among his rags, and she wished he would go away. But going away was not part of his intention. He slowly brought out a large iron spoon and, to the vexation of the woman, knelt down on the ground and peered into the pot. Then he gave his reply.

"When Christ is near, water becomes wine;" and with that he skimmed the simmering liquid and lifted a spoonful to his mouth.

"It's tasty," said he; "awfully tasty—really amazingly tasty."

Anna smiled and answered simply, "I'm glad you like it, grandfather." Grandfather took another spoonful and smacked his lips. "You know," said he, "this is something quite out of the way; it is very original; I knew it was very good soup, it was speaking so well. I heard its voice far away. It called to me, it sang. What do you say to it, my dear, if I dine with you to-night?"

Anna looked up at him appealingly. "No," said she, "pass by. We are very poor, and this is all we have to eat; it is too poor for any guest. Dear old man, go away."

"Oh, no! I don't think so. This sort of soup a king would be glad to eat. It is the sort kings can't get. You might even make a great fortune if you sent a sealed tin of this to the Tsar. The Tsar's cook is a great friend of mine; if you could get on the right side of him you'd never want for a piece of meat to throw in the soup. But I advise you, don't part with the recipe, it's worth its weight in gold. And now, what do you say to having me as a boarder? Yes, surely as God rules over everything why shouldn't I stay here? How much shall I pay? Well, never mind, you make this soup each day and then you can save all the money."

Anna now felt seriously troubled. An old ragged man could be no help to her; he could not pay her anything, and she would be poorer than before. She pinched up her pretty lips into a bunch, and frowned and shook her head violently; it would never do. "No, grandfather, I couldn't take you; we are very poor, and you are even poorer than we are."

Thereupon the old man laughed exuberantly, and his eyes shone like those of Santa Claus.

"I know, I know, I know," said he.

"What do you know, grandfather?"

The old man laughed again, and then pulled out a large volume, old and rusty-leaved. It was a Bible, and he opened it between the Old Testament and the New, and there were money notes for seven hundred roubles.

"That's what," said he. "My wages for clearing the

clouds out of the sky for the Sultan of Turkey—for you twelve roubles a month, and you needn't spend a penny of it, for we shall live on such soup as this."

Anna meekly bade him welcome, wondering who he might be in disguise. Some great man, surely, she thought, for he seemed very highly connected.

"What is your name, grandfather?" said she, as he stumped into her room and sat down on the box, and took little Foma on one knee and Mania on the other.

"What is my name?" said he. "Ho, ho, ho," and he laughed. "That's a good joke. It is a long, long while since anyone asked me my name. I've heard so many names; they were so like mine that I got confused long ago, and it wasn't worth while remembering. What do you think, little Fomitchka? And you'll be asking where I come from. Really, I don't know. How many provinces are there in Russia? Thousands surely. One day I slipped out of my own province and lost myself, and I kept coming to new provinces, always new names, and the places just looked the same. You know it says in the Bible Adam was the first man; Mr Adam, then came Mr Cain Adam and Mr Abel Adam, and Mr Seth Adam. You call me Mr Adam."

"A-dam, grandpa," said little Foma.

So the ragged old man with the money and the Bible and the spoon came and lived with them. They all lived together, slept in the same room, and ate from the same table. Every morning Anna went to the market with her pot and collected food, and every evening she boiled soup on the stones, whilst grandfather dipped his finger or his spoon into the stew and tasted it approvingly. Every Sunday she received three roubles from him and put them by. It was strange; they lived as poorly now as they had done before. So poorly they lived that they only had tea once a week, and they boiled it in a saucepan and had it without sugar. Grandfather had produced a partly-used two-ounce packet of tea from his overcoat. Yet this tea-party was something glorious—a strange weekly happiness to be anticipated even six days ahead. Anna ceased to feel anxious, and the children grew rounder and happier, though it was difficult to see how it had come to be. They were being fed by something more than soup; perhaps, as they scrambled about grandfather's knees and listened to his stories, they were enchanted a little. Anna looked at them and wondered. Grandfather has tramped through sun and rain, thought she—how dark and rich his hands are, like the black earth in the spring. Her little baby, that had done nothing but scream and look unhappy since it was born, had now begun to smile. It smiled at grandfather like a little evening gleam of sunshine after wet, wet days.

"Lizetchka," her mother would exclaim. "Ah, Lizetchka! Little Lizetchka! My little angel!" Then the neighbours came in and they would have found fault and gossiped, but grandfather's cheery way took their hearts by surprise. And the owner of the cottage, who was responsible, wanted to turn the old man out because he had no passport, and it was dangerous to harbour such a man; but he, too, was won over; though he was mean, and had a wife meaner than himself, he contentedly took the risk. Sometimes his wife would urge him on against Anna and the old man, and he would go to them to say stern words; but when he came and saw the children, with their little fingers tangled in grandfather's hair, he would forget his message and laugh and say, " Ah, Mr Adam! Fancy you living here without a passport! It's all right living so, eh? "

So time went on, and no one disturbed the little *ménage* of Anna and her three children and Mr Adam. Years passed, and the old man ceased to be a surprise; nothing new happened; no one inquired after him; no one claimed him. He lived all the while in his rags, and read from his Bible, and played with the children, and praised the soup, and made merry with the neighbours. Only once Anna had been sad. That was when she mended his torn red shirt for him. She had often mended Peter's clothes whilst he wore them on his body, and now an irresistible memory brought back the pathos of her loss. She wept a little and Adam comforted her, and as she looked through her tears at him she felt suddenly very grateful, and it seemed to her that perhaps Peter had sent this man to her to help her. Suddenly the thanks which had been mounting up in her heart overflowed, and as she finished sewing she put her arms round his neck and kissed him.

The days of these years were strange days, the strangest of Anna's life, and in after years they seemed only a few days, only a short, strange period of heavenly comfort. For the time came when she had Adam no more. He fell ill and died.

" Mr Adam's dead," said all the neighbours, and they felt very sad. " Mr Adam is dead," said the owner's wife. " Now you'll see how foolish it is to have a man without a passport. What will the police say? You'll have to put his dead body in a field for men to find, and then it will be said we murdered him."

" Grandpa dead," said all the children and moped.

But Anna felt very troubled. What was she to do with him, a man without a name, without a family, without a village? A man who had over five hundred roubles in his Bible! Poor Anna! Had she but had a little cunning she might have put by those five hundred roubles to be a little fortune for herself. Grandfather had died very suddenly or he would have told her to do so. Anna was simple enough to go and tell the police her story, and an official came, looked at the man, and took away the Bible, saying he would have it examined. In the Bible lay the precious notes! Then Anna bought white robes and took off Adam's rags, and washed his body, and laid him upon some clean boards, and bought a cheap coffin, and hired a man to dig a grave, and she went and buried him, and put a little Ikon on his breast, and held a lighted candle over his tomb, and sang the thrice-holy hymn, " Holy, holy, holy," and went home. Adam was no more; they were poor; the official never returned with the Bible; no one asked about the missing passport. But what the greedy official had not guessed, and what Adam had never divulged, was that in his rags, in one of his many deep pockets, was secreted another sum of money, a thousand roubles. This Anna found, and was wiser than before, having learnt from experience. To-day she keeps a little cookshop and is prosperous, and the peasants say that she, better than any of the wives of the village, knows how to make good soup.

Such was the story the tramp told me. He liked telling it, and now, as I have repeated it, I find the same personality in the friend of the woman and in my acquaintance. Surely Adam did not really die. Adam never really dies.

One other thing he said to me that remains; there are two Adams—the Adam before he tasted the fruit and the Adam after he had tasted. Most Russians retain their Eden happiness, but whenever one of them tastes of the Tree of Knowledge his old happiness is cursed; the time has come for him to leave Eden and seek the new happiness. Adam was the first *modern* man. The tramps have found the second Eden.

CHAPTER XXIX

THE BAPTIST CHAPEL

I HAVE continually come across Protestants in Russia. They are undoubtedly increasing in numbers very rapidly. Several times when I was out in the mountains I came across proselytising Baptists and Molokans. The Molokan is a sect of Protestant exclusively Russian, I think. They differ from orthodox peasants by their ethics. They hold it a sin to smoke or to drink, and they do not recognise the Ikons. Even in Lisitchansk there had been a Baptist family, and in Moscow I had found Lutherans.

M. Stolypin's ukase marked the decease of Pan-Slavism, that policy summarised in the words—one Tsar, one Tongue, one Church. It was comparatively little noticed, this Emancipation Bill of Russia, but it will probably prove a more important concession to the forces of Democracy than any other fruit of the Revolutionary struggle. It began a new era: historians in the future will take it as a starting-point in the history of Russian freedom. Meanwhile, despite rumours to the contrary, Russia as a whole is as peaceful as Bedfordshire. The Revolutionary storm has passed away; the new issues of life and death germinate in silence. The flushed red fruit burst out, the seeds were scattered. To-day the seeds gather strength and grow and put forth shoots, and even the ordinary observer is aware of the beginning of a crop whose nature is sufficiently enigmatical. On another day there will be another harvest. And if Elizabethan Puritans meant ultimately the Whitehall gallows, one may ask apprehensively for the significance of the Puritanism that is springing into existence in the reign of Nicholas II.

I was talking to the pastor one evening shortly after I came.

"We increase, brother," said he to me, "we increase. Three years ago there were only 120 of us and now we are 300; in three more years we shall be half a thousand, not less."

"But is it not dangerous?" I said. "Surely you come into conflict with the authorities."

"Not much now. Three of us were hanged two years ago. And often meetings are forbidden. The last Governor forbade our meetings altogether; that was ten years ago. Many of us suffered through that; some are in prison now and some died in prison. But we held our meetings despite the ukase of the Governor. We used to gather together at a friend's house, and then after tea we would have our few hymns and a prayer or two. These meetings were generally very happy, the common bond of danger made us closer than brothers."

" And you? " I asked. " Were you ever arrested? "

" Yes, with four others one night; two of them died in prison, they were old men and it was hard on them. I served five years' penal servitude. That was for holding a meeting against the order."

The minister was silent as if recalling old memories, and then suddenly he went on as if brushing aside his thoughts. " But things are quieter now. In all Russia there are twenty thousand Baptists alone, besides many thousand other Protestants, and we are added to in numbers every year. In Rostof a little congregation has become three thousand since the Duma came in. And now dotted all over the country we have little missions among the peasants; it's the peasants who're coming to us, and nobody else has been able to teach them. Every year new missions start. Next month I make my little country tour, when the harvesters are in the fields, and I go to five new places—five places to which the Gospel has come this year."

On the very first Sunday morning comes my host to warn me not to be late for service. I prepared to go to chapel seriously; it was long since I had been in any place of worship other than a temple of the Orthodox Church.

Half a mile distant I found the building, the little defiant, heterodox place so brave in its denial and protest. Here was no church, not even a chapel, just a plain wooden building. This black, gaunt building, less beautiful and less ornamented than a house. God dwells in those jewelled, perfumed caskets of the Orthodox Church; He dwells here also. How well and how daringly the paradox had been asserted! And they called it a meeting, not a service, and it was held up-stairs and not down; and instead of standing all through one sat all through, and there were no crosses and no ornaments and no collections, and the women sat on one side while the men sat on the other.

The room was large. Wooden forms ranged on each side, there was a narrow passage down the middle, and at the head of it stood the preacher's platform, slightly elevated from the people. The whole looked somewhat like a chapel schoolroom.

The congregation was in its way quite a grand one. Not that it was by any means numerous; the little place was full, one couldn't say more than that. But there wasn't a woman dressed in anything finer than printed cotton, and the minister was the only man who wore a collar. Something in the people called out one's reverence. Each woman had a cotton shawl for head-dress, and as the women's side filled one looked along a vista of shawled heads, and when now and then one of them turned to look at a stranger one saw the broad-browed, pale face of a peasant woman.

They were all peasant folk, or working men or artisans,

and very simple and earnest. One knew much of them when one heard the words of their elected pastor. Ivan Savelev, when he came in, walked directly to his place and knelt, and then after a few minutes' silence closed his prayer by a few words spoken on behalf of the congregation—gentle, simple words, such as a mother might put into the mouth of her child. He is a tall, douce man, the minister, of a Scottish type of countenance. His calm face and eyes suggest an infinite reserve of wisdom, and his gentle, musical voice tells of a mind and will in harmony. Presently he read from the Bible, and then gave out a hymn, and afterwards spoke from a text, first to the women, then to the men, and then to both collectively, and then gave out another hymn. What struck me was that he did each thing as if it were worth while, so that the numbers of the hymns sounded beautifully.

The people sang with a will and kept in tune. The pastor, after giving out the number, stepped over to the harmonium and played a tune. He is choir-master as well as preacher, and teaches his people new tunes from two books of his own—*Hymns, Ancient and Modern,* and an old copy of *Moody and Sankey;* priceless treasures, one would say, though the printed English words remain inscrutable. We went off to the tune of " See the conquering hero comes," the Russian words seeming very irrelevant. When the tune was in full swing one really felt oneself back in England—old memories crowded to my mind. Just before the sermon there was another hymn, and this to the tune of " Oh, God, our help in ages past;" but a presto motif, and a quaint alteration in the phrasing of the tune, reminded one of peals of church bells. They sang it as if the lines ran:

> " Oh, God, our help in ages past our
> Hope for years to come.
> Our Shelter from the stormy blast and
> Our Eternal home."

The pastor's sermon was direct; to him the issue was clear. Not alone those who say "*Gospody, Gospody,*" but those who do the will of my Father shall enter into the Kingdom. He counselled them to lead earnest, sober lives, and to bring up their families in the truth. Everyone listened in resolute stillness. One felt their God in the midst of them—the God of the Puritans.

I found my thoughts straying back to England, and I wondered if I saw before me a picture of what the early Independents or early Methodists were like. I was accustomed to chapels in London where each person belongs to our advanced civilisation, and where the preacher hands more than the simple bread of life. Here each man was of the crude, rough material out of which civilisations are made. Here was a passion for simplicity; everything was elemental, original. There were strange, new silences to be divined below the voices and the sounds, strange barenesses and nakednesses underneath the scanty nature of the service. For a moment one shut one's eyes to the room, and opened other eyes to another scene—to the stable and the manger and the straw. Yes, here were the beginnings of things.

After service I walked home with the pastor. " You will become a political force," I said. " Who knows ? " he replied. " I hope not, but we increase in numbers. Everyone added to us is one added to the forces of truth and purity."

Some pilgrims passed us. " There they go," he said, " hundred of miles to pray to God in an ancient monastery. God is there, He is not here, so they say. They go to pray, and they waste their money and their time, and it all ends in vodka drinking. God grant they may become less and less."

The pilgrims retreated, staff in hand, hooded and with great bundles on their backs. Slowly, as it were, reluctantly, they moved away, and to me they seemed the living figure of the past, and this fresh, strong man beside me was the new.

" You are laying the foundation of a Russian democracy," I went on. " In England or America you would see a democracy three hundred years ahead of this. Have you heard of the London slums, or of Chicago? Are you not afraid of the responsibility? "

He smiled. " Three hundred years is a long time,

brother. We teach the truth. If your people have gone wrong it was because they turned away, they took wrong turnings. It is God's will that we preach and spread the truth."

Ivan Savelev carried himself with the air of one who had uttered an unquestionable truism. His truths were his own, and for him indisputable. I left him and went to meditate on the secret life I had discovered.

It moves silently and unseen, like running water under snow, and on countless hillsides and valleys and plains the spring movement has begun. One day Russia will awake and find the season new. Then there will come another autumn and another harvest, and the good seed will be found to have multiplied thirtyfold, sixtyfold, and some an hundredfold.

DEVDORAK GLACIER, GORGE OF DARIEL

CHAPTER XXX

THE WOMAN WHO SAW GOD

ONE day, when I was visiting a village on the steppes, I came upon a strange comedy very typical of Russian life. I went in to a bootmaker to get one of my boots sewn up, and I overheard the following conversation.

" Marya Petrovna has seen the Anti-Christ," says the cobbler's wife.

" No," says Jeremy, her husband, " it is God who has looked on her. God has been very pleased with Masha."

" Yes," rejoins his wife, " she seems very holy, but I don't like it. Last Sunday at church she knelt so long that everyone thought she had fallen asleep. When the priest opened the door of the church she went in and knelt down on the stones before the blessed Ikon. All through the service she kneeled, and all through the Communion, and though she had bought her loaf and the priest called her she did not go up to the altar, but simply went on kneeling. Then, when the bells rang and we all went out, she still remained kneeling. And she didn't cross herself. The priest himself had to come and lift her out of the church so that he could lock up. I think she's under a curse. She has done some dreadful sin — has talked with wood spirits, perhaps."

" The Squire's son came on the Devil's hoof marks in the forest last week, and saw a man with eight dead foxes shortly afterwards."

The cobbler's wife held up her hands with horror.

Katusha, a young woman from a neighbouring izba, has come in.

" You speak of Marya Petrovna," says she. " We saw her last night, Tanya, Lida and I and a lot of us looking through the window. She was kneeling on her knees and praying to the samovar and calling it God. The priest went in and tried to talk with her, and he tried to raise her, but it was difficult, so he picked up the samovar instead and hid it away. Then poor Masha stood up, and we saw her look at the big black pot that has the cabbage soup in it, and she crossed herself as if it were an Ikon. Two days, they say, she hasn't eaten, and Peter, her husband, has had to get his meals himself. She won't do anything in the house, and directly she sees something new she goes down on her knees to it. The priest has been reasoning with her, and she says she sees God everywhere. God is everywhere, that is true, but Masha says He's in the pots and pans and in the stove, and she won't sit on a chair because she says it's all God. You should have seen her last night, she looked a holy saint, and her eyes were full of light."

" Lord save us! " exclaimed the cobbler's wife.

" Permit me to go on. Her eyes were full of light, and she lifted up her hands to the roof, and sang strange music, so that we all felt terrified, and the priest wept. When we saw the priest weeping we didn't know what to think, and presently he and Peter came and told us to go home, and that Marya Petrovna had had a vision —God had been so good to her."

The cobbler looked very solemnly at her for some minutes, and then turned his gaze upon his wife. " I think," said he, " that it may be that this is the second coming of Christ."

" Idiot! " exclaimed his wife. " How could Masha be Christ? "

" I don't mean Masha," he replied, " but perhaps she sees Him coming. He may be getting nearer and nearer every moment, and Masha may see the glory brighter and brighter. Masha always was our most religious."

At this point the grocer's wife, in a red petticoat and a jacket and a shawl, rushed in, and exclaimed:

" Just think, friends, Marya Petrovna is dead! I am absolutely the first person to give the news, I had it from the priest just as he left the house. He watched with her all night—but pardon me, I must be going."

With that she rushed out to be the first to give the news to the rest of the village.

The cobbler and his wife exclaimed together, "Bozhe moï! Oh, Lord!" And Katusha slipped out after the grocer's wife, intending evidently to have her share in the glory of gossip. The cobbler threw aside his last, and went out as he was, in his apron and without his hat, and his wife went with him. They swelled the little crowd that was already collected outside Masha's dwelling.

It was indeed as the grocer's wife had indicated. Marya Petrovna had died. Of what she had died everyone could say something. Some peasants ascribed it to the Devil and some to God. The majority held that God had taken her to heaven. The priest's explanation was that the woman's life had been very acceptable to God, and that He had blesed her with a vision of His glory. The vision had been a promise; it had perhaps shown her her glorious place in heaven. The vision of God had entered her eyes, so that she could not put it aside and look at the ordinary things of life. She could not see a samovar—she saw God. She couldn't make tea with the samovar; that would have been sacrilege. She could not eat soup, she couldn't sit down, she couldn't lie down, she couldn't touch anything. To do these things was sacrilege. So she died. She died from utter exhaustion and from starvation. No doubt God had taken this means to bring her from the world.

Such was the story that the priest communicated to

his superiors and to St Petersburg, hoping that it might perhaps be thought fit to honour the mortal memory of this new Mary whom the Lord had honoured. No canonisation, however, followed, though to the inhabitants of the village of Celo the woman remains a saint and a wonder, and the moujiks cross themselves as they pass the cottage where she used to live.

CHAPTER XXXI

ALI PASHA

THE Persian nation, which numbers seven or eight millions of dwellers on its own soil, has many thousands scattered over the rich valleys of the Caucasus. In Tiflis, in Baku, Batum, Kutais, the Persian, clad in vermilion or crimson or slate-blue, is a familiar figure in the streets. Their wares, their inlaid guns and swords and belts, their rugs and cloaks, are the glory of all the bazaars of Trans-Caucasia. One's eye rests with pleasure on their leisurely movements, their gentle forms and open, courteous gait; and they give an atmosphere of peace and serenity to streets where otherwise the knives of hillmen, and the sullen accoutrements of Cossacks, would continually impress one with the notion of impending storm.

Ali Pasha, or, as his friends familiarly call him, Ali Khan, is one of this gentle, harassed nation, a native of Ararat, having been brought up within the shadow of that awful mountain upon which, it is said, the Ark first grounded.

I had my first talk with him one evening shortly

after I came to the mill. It was a Saturday night, and the pastor's family were preparing for the Sabbath by holding a prayer-meeting round the samovar. The other neighbours were skulking round the window listening to the hymn-singing, so we were left to ourselves.

It was in the shade of evening. He was having his tea at his ease—crimson tea, coloured by infusion of cranberry syrup. I was sitting near by, writing a letter to England. He looked over with some interest, and presently came and stood over me, regarding my fountain pen and English caligraphy with a mild curiosity. I gave him the pen to examine, he handled it carefully, and, having eyed it over with naïve amazement, returned it in silence. He volunteered to show me Persian writing, and presently brought forth from his dwelling two volumes of prayers written in what was evidently Persian copper-plate, and by his own hand. Each word, though symmetrical in itself, looked like a pen-and-ink sketch of a wood on fire in a wind. Yet it was very beautiful and reminiscent of nothing so much as of an old Bible copied before the days of printing.

Ali Khan had purple beard and hair—his head looks as if it had been soaked in black-currant juice. His face is smoky, his eyes grey, benignant. He wears a slate-blue cloak, golden stockings, and loose slippers; he is slender, and stands some five feet ten above the ground. His finger nails and the palms of his hands are carmined.

He had never met an Englishman before, and eyed me somewhat incredulously when I said I came from London. " The English are a wonderful people," he remarked. " Their ships call at all the ports of the world, the armies of the great Queen are more countless than the stars of heaven." I explained that the Queen was dead, and that we had a King now, but the Persian's interests seemed to be little in foreign affairs, and he was all eager to tell me of his prayers and fasts. No, he was not a Babi, but a pure Mahommedan. There were sects of Mahommedans, just as many as there were Christian sects. His church was up on the hill, the one with the crescent moons on the spires. Soon a big fast would commence, and he must eat no food during seventeen hours each day.

I ventured to pronounce the words " Omar Khayyám. He smiled, but did not seem surprised that I had heard of him. " Our Omar." Yes, he read Omar. " And do your people read Omar much? " I asked. " It is in vain," he replied; " my people are very wretched, few can read, and few care to. It is noble to be on horseback fighting with the Russians, or against the Russians. No; boys used to go to school, but now they run wild, for there is such disorder."

A sort of sweet melancholy came over his face, and I asked him how he came to be an exile from his country. " It is not a bad country to be exiled from," he began. " It would have been in vain if I had remained there.

Ali Mamedof wrote to me to come here, that there were many of my countrymen here, and there were plenty who wanted coats. So I came by the train to Tiflis, and then in a wagon through the mountain passes." He told me how he was taught in a little Persian school in Ararat, that when he was twelve years old he had left school and taken a hand in his father's workshop and helped to weave Persian rugs. I pictured the large open doorway of the booth, the two at work squatting on carpet stools before the high bamboo frame on which the thing of wonder was being wrought, the peacock in it, the half-finished peacock perhaps, with gigantic tail, coming into being among living crimsons and lambent blues, brilliant scarlets and lurid yellows.

His father had been taken off by typhus before the youngster had experience enough to be able to carry on the business by himself; the mother had died long since, so Ali was left an orphan. He got work from a tailor, and sat in a little room with him, and worked all day with assiduity not less than that of the sweated journeyman of England. But things mended, and Ali Khan got orders of his own, and bought his own Singer sewing-machine and his own cloth and black sheepskin, and then in a little wooden room of his own squatted on his own carpet, and lived in independence many a happy year.

Then the Russians had come. They built their railway even right alongside the sacred mountain, and connected Ararat with Tiflis and Batum and Baku, and, indeed, with all the North. Rugs and swords went to Tiflis by train instead of by camel, and ready-made trousers and cast-off clothes came back in exchange. Then with the ready-made trousers came the Russian trader, and the almost ubiquitous German commercial traveller. Russians and Caucasians came in, and Russian officials and Cossacks, Russian police and passports. Ali's trade grew bad. His Russian customers were hard to please, the prospect of war and massacre was what all the natives talked of, and many of his friends and customers had been called away to fight at Tabriz and Teheran. Ali Khan had looked despairingly at the future. Then Ali Mamedof had written, and he had taken his advice.

He came and settled up in this territory, indubitably Russian, though on the mountains, and found to his surprise some thousands of his countrymen there. "Would you not rather be in Persia?" I asked. "Oh, no," he rejoined. "There is no security there, and there is no money there. Ours is a poor country, and is full of enemies. Here is much custom. I shall grow rich, and perhaps afterwards, when things are quieter, I shall return to Ararat, to spend my old age there."

"And the Shah?" I asked. "Oh, they've caught him," he replied. "He'll come and live in the Caucasus also. It is much better for him."

At this point he began to put his samovar up. It

was nearing the daily prayer time. He went leisurely into his dwelling again and shut the windows, and passed into his inner room, where a square carpet lay.

Presently I heard the faint sound of his voice. I pictured him, as he was no doubt, kneeling on his carpet, praying in the words of his hand-written volumes to the one God—praying for the time of peace for Persia, and for all the world, and at the same time resigned and gentle before the Eternal Will.

So my acquaintance began with Ali Pasha. I think he was a noble man, and by far the most refined and courteous of the dwellers at the mill. I might almost add, though it would sound paradoxical, he was the most Christian. Nowadays surely all men are Christian, even Mahommedans, Buddhists and Confucians. It is only the name that they lack, the same religion is in all of them.

There was a woman near by who worked at a brewery and worked very hard, although she drank too much. Alimka and Fatima were her children, and they were so starved that they would rob the chickens of the waste food thrown in the yard. I noticed that Ali lent the woman money and helped her with the children. And when a Punch and Judy show came into the yard Ali subscribed more generously than anyone else so that the children might have a treat. And when I took little Jason under my care Ali backed me up. He even tried to rescue another bird and pass it on to me.

But he was very punctilious in the performance of the services of his own religion. Special praying men came in to pray for him at different times during the summer, and their loud keening sounded in my ears long after I had gone to bed. Then when the Feast of Ramazan came he lived the life of a hermit.

CHAPTER XXXII

THE SORROWING MAN

A WOMAN in Vladikavkaz, being told she could not live long, grew so much in love with the idea of death that she ordered her coffin in advance, and lay in it in her bedroom and had a mock funeral, just to see what it felt like. That was an incident rather typical of the life of the *intelligentia* of the place. There are many nerveless, sad, despairing people there, people with no apparent means of happiness, people of morbid imagination and a will to be unhappy. All around them Nature has outdone herself with seductive charm; the sun flashes on the mountains, the myriad flowers smile in the valleys, the happy peasantry flood the town with jovial, laughing faces, but all in vain. "The fact is," as I said to Ivan Savilief, "Adam was only the first modern man; the peasants are still living in their Edens. All your modern Adam and Eves have got to get saved somehow." The Baptist, who, it must be remembered, was still a peasant, and by no means one of the educated classes, was very happy. And his notion was that the sad people needed to believe; they needed faith.

They got as near to happiness as it was possible for them. They got as far as feet could carry them, but for the last gulf they needed wings.

Here is a story of a Russian man, one who failed to accomplish his happiness.

A certain man had great possessions and great happiness. He had inherited broad lands and gold; he was young and strong and able to enjoy riches; and he had friends and the good opinion of the world. The cup of his happiness was broad and deep and brimming. Behold what happened to him; there came a time when he achieved the summit of earthly bliss, and then suddenly he lost all and became a man of sorrow.

He was a good man. He had kept the laws of God and of man; no one could reproach him. His mind was young and fresh and open to the influences of beauty. His heart and mind were in communion. God looked upon him and smiled, and then suddenly there came a time when, as it were, God turned away His face.

This is the story of the change. The man's life, with its wealth and its adornment, its pillars and its towers, its sumptuous chambers and domes of pleasure was as a precious palace just completed. Within the hall the glories of his youth lay, the crowns and the laurels, the shields and the swords. They were cast there, and upon all there was erected a throne. And then the most beautiful maiden his world could give was seated upon the throne. The palace as perfection throbbed—dared to exist. The young man realised for a minute the dizziest heights of happiness.

But on his marriage eve he fell.

It had been a saying of his boyhood that the condition of happiness is that one follow unfalteringly one's highest hope. It had always seemed to him that Hope must go on before, that however happy one became there would always be the prospect of further happiness, that one never could catch up hope. And now, behold, he stood *at one* with his ideal, and he felt that earth had no more to give.

On his marriage eve he communed with his heart, and having given thanks to God, as was his wont, he fell into a trance. For a space time ceased to exist for him, whilst his soul was borne away from him to unknown powers. When he awoke he was changed. The trouble and doubt that excess of joy had brought him had given way to a sort of exaltation. His light blue eyes were gentle, as if they had looked long upon the soft plumage of wings, and there was a strange radiance within them. It was the light of inspiration, the gleam of the knowledge of God. He walked as one might, having news of a great deliverance.

" The condition of happiness is that one follow unfalteringly one's highest hope," said he. " And when one comes level with one's highest hope, God will destroy the old hope and give a new one. There is a dark moment at the summit of one's mountain, and then suddenly, when the last inch upward is achieved, God gives His perfect revelation. The old cup of happiness is dashed to pieces on the rocks when one sees the Grail."

It had come to the knowledge of the man that a greater joy than that afforded by earthly things was possible. He dimly apprehended the coming of a new fortune, of a new opportunity. Some voice within him seemed to cry, "Behold *the* opportunity comes; the white horse comes riding past your gate; jump on it and ride away! Something comes for which this present happiness is only a preparation. There comes an adventure worth your sword, and a true bride for your heart. There is a narrow portal to be reached, and now, even now, riseth the tide which takes you there. Only once in a lifetime comes the tide that lifts you and puts you on the high seas."

What did it mean?

He knelt and communed with his heart. He tried to understand the Voice which spoke to him. He composed his fluttering spirit, and then prayed to God. He prayed, "What must I do, oh, God, to win eternal joy?" He prayed and waited, and his soul grew calm as a broad lake at eve. There came no answer to his prayer, but whilst he waited he became conscious of a new power. The deep silence of the world seemed to have congealed, and before him stood a great grey door.

" For each man there is a door to happiness," said the voice in his heart; " the door is shut, but the key is in the door."

" Yes, the key is in the door," said he. " I could not have seen the key had I not power to open."

Suddenly, in the calm of his heart, the young man willed to behold God and to attain supreme joy, and he knew that the Vision would be vouchsafed to him. But just as he was about to see that which he desired to behold, the Devil, in the shape of a crow, flew across the sky of his soul and alighted in his heart. The lake at eve was ruffled, and a whisper like a cold night breeze from the east sped along the surface of it and said, " You will find the true bride for your heart, but does not that mean you must renounce this earthly beauty who has just crowned the happiness of your youth? You will become as a little child and begin life again, and forego all the honour that your years and wealth have brought you. If you see God once, nothing less than God will ever satisfy you, and your eyes, having looked on that radiance, will find the world intolerably grey."

Then a great terror sprang up in him like two contrary winds born together in a wood, and it shook his spirit. His soul was stirred up from the bottom so that it lost all its purity, and he prayed, " Oh, Lord, do not show thyself lest nothing hereafter give me joy: it is my will, take this cup from me." The prayer was heard, and the white robe of his transfiguration was caught up into the heavens again.

He saw not the Vision.

He saw not the Vision, but since that day he cannot be satisfied by anything other than it.

So it happened that on his marriage eve he fell from the dizzy heights of happiness and became a man of sorrow. He passed, as it were, out of the favour of God. His estate decayed a little, but even the great wealth which remained was but barren gold. His mind and body grew infirm. With his bride he had no happiness. He lost the good opinion of the world, and those who once were friends pointed at him and said, " There goes a failure, a man not yet of middle age, but disillusioned and crusty."

The man is now spending the rest of his days and he goes sadly indeed. No other opportunity has come, and he knows in himself he will never be so near again. He has become a lonely man, one who prefers his own company, and likes to look upon the sky, or at the wild things in the woods. He always appears as if he were looking for something he has lost. His eyes are wistful and sorrow-charged, his step heavy, his thoughts slow. He comes nearest to happiness on cloudy days of autumn when he attunes himself to Nature. Then he has quiet moments and little pleasures, and accidentally looking at some mouse or shrew scurrying among the yellow leaves, he laughs to himself or smiles a little.

Then suddenly one might see him check himself as he catches sight of the red October sun or some dark, threatening cloud. He remembers his renunciation, his supreme denial, and is again appalled. Conscience and life will not let him forget, and he sees ever before him the reverse side of the great silent door—the door which is locked, but for which there is no key. . . .

The man searches, the man waits. He is like a ghost that may not rest, until a mistake of the old has been set right in the new. Men become his enemies. He desperately hates the circumstances of life, the things that made up his former happiness. The face in the picture hates the frame which does not suit.

Is it not all in vain! The lost opportunity never returns; the tide never rises the second time; the White Horse never comes past the gate again. " It is easier for a camel to pass through the eye of a needle than for a rich man to enter the Kingdom of Heaven." " With man it is impossible, but with God all things are possible."

CHAPTER XXXIII

THE CUCUMBER FAIR

THE cost of living in the Caucasus is one-half of what it is in the most thriving agricultural district in Great Britain. This is because Russia is a self-supporting empire; it does not depend on other countries for its food supply. I think the comparative economic positions of England and Russia are inadequately known. In England the land has been sacrificed to manufactures; by adopting Free Trade it made a bargain with other countries in these terms—that it would manufacture iron goods and cloth in exchange for food. It gave up agriculture and it gave up the country. It became a land of towns. The people of the English towns *are* the English people. Russia, on the other hand, remained an agricultural country, and its manufactures have developed little. It is content to take foreign manufactured goods in exchange for its own superfluous food. The people of Russia are the peasants; the Liberals in the towns don't really count. For town life and factory life democracy is most suitable, and for country life conservatism and squiredom—for English people democracy, for Russians autocracy.

"TURNING OVER COTTONS"

AN OSSETINE VILLAGE

Those in England who have a strong wish to have Russia democratised are also, strange to say, Free Traders. Are they aware that if Russia becomes a manufacturing country it will need its food for itself, and will not need to buy our wares? Russia is really the employer of England. What if England loses its job?

The newspaper boom of the revolution has done much harm; it has given English people a false idea of Russia. That notion of Russia as a place of anarchists and *gendarmes*, secret societies, spies, plots, prisons is ridiculous. As after the Slaves War the Romans lined the way home by poles on which the heads of the conquered were fixed, so to the ordinary outsider appears the boundary line of Russia—a palisade of heads on poles. In truth, it is only fenced in by passport officers, unless the outworks of lies in the European press must be counted. Behind the fence, however, stands, not what so many imagine—cossacks, cannon, prisons—but an extraordinarily fertile, fruitful country, and a people happy enough to be unaware of their happiness or unhappiness. I have spoken to peasants from all parts of the country, and I have not found one who had a word to say against the Tsar, or who felt any grievance against his country's governors.

There are a hundred millions of peasants who swear by God and the Tsar, and who believe implicitly in both God and Tsar, a hundred million strong, healthy peasants, not yet taught to read or write, not yet democratised and given a vote, not yet crammed to death in manufacturing towns. These are Europe's unspent capital, her little store of unspoiled men set against a rainy day, the solid wall between China and the West.

It was with these thoughts uppermost in my mind that I came away from one of the July fairs at Vladikavkaz. Such revelations of the bounty of Nature in the abundance of food, and in strong limbs to be nourished by it, I scarcely expect to see easily again. This fair took place at one end of the great military road that traverses the Caucasus, and connects Tiflis and the Persian marches with Rostof and the North. In a great open square, paved unevenly with cobbles, the stalls are set up. At one end are five open forges, where horses are strapped in and shod. Behind these, about a hundred sheep and lambs struggle together, whilst a shepherd milks the ewes into a bucket. At another end of the "bazaar" there is a covered place for cotton goods, and there the Georgian girl buys her kerchief, and the peasant woman turns over all manner of brilliant printed cotton. Between the sheep and the drapery, for a full hundred yards, stand carts and barrows, or, it may be, merely sacks and baskets, full of cucumbers and tomatoes. The cucumbers are piled up on the carts like loads of stones for road-making. The vendors stand beside them and shout their prices. The customers fumble about and pick out the best they can find of the stock. Behind or below the stalls the rotten ones lie yellow and soft under the burning sun, and hens come in and peck at them. Several thousand have to be sold before afternoon; more than half will not be disposed of before they are spoiled by the sun. Picture the peasants outbidding one another, fat and perspiring in the heat. Ten for three-halfpence is the highest price, ten for a halfpenny the lowest. By two o'clock in the afternoon one will be able to buy forty for a penny, just to clear. Meanwhile children are dancing about, eating them as one would bananas in England, munching them as if they were large pears, and in a way that would have brought bewilderment to the mind of Sairey Gamp, who so dearly loved a "cowcumber." A fortnight ago a single cucumber cost twopence—assuredly the tide has risen.

Scarcely less in evidence than the luscious green of cucumbers is the reposing yellow and scarlet of the tomatoes—golden apples they call them. These also must be disposed of; they go for a penny a pound, and the baskets of many traffickers are adorned by the purchase of them. Behind the cucumber row is the potato market, where, for sixpence, you may buy two stone of new potatoes. With these are a long array of stalls with vegetables and fruit, everything superabundant, and at surprising prices. Raspberries and apricots go at twopence a pound, peaches at fourpence, cherries and plums at a penny, gooseberries at a halfpenny, blackberries at three-halfpence, and all this fruit in at the same time. Strawberries came suddenly at the beginning of June, and as suddenly disappeared; the summer progresses at quick pace here. New-laid eggs are sold at this fair at a farthing each, cheese at threepence a pound, butter at tenpence, bacon at fourpence and fivepence a pound. Herrings and river fish, sundried and cured, are sold ten on a string for twopence halfpenny; live green crayfish, ten for threepence. At shops near by, mutton is sold at threepence halfpenny, and lamb at fourpence halfpenny a pound; beef at threepence.

The fair is, however, a poor people's market. The richer get their things at the shops, but it is difficult to persuade a peasant to buy at a shop when he can get what he wants at a fair. From time immemorial the country people have met and bargained at fairs, so that it is now in the blood. Hence it is that Russia is the country of fairs, having as its greatest object of that kind the fair of Nizhni Novgorod, that stupendous revival of the old times. The difficulty of buying at a fair is no obstacle; the crowds of people, the mountebanks among them, the stalls without scales, the haphazard bargains, and chance of bad money, are more alluring than deterrent. Potatoes are sold by the pailful, cucumbers by the ten, fish by the string, bacon and cheese by the piece, and mutton mostly by the sheep. One needs to be a connoisseur, a ready calculator and eye-measurer, if one is going to acquit oneself honourably in the eyes of the fair bargain-drivers. No one ever takes anything at the price offered; everyone chaffers and bargains for at least five minutes before settling yes or no. Then nothing bought is wrapped up. One has to bring one's own paper with one, or one may buy earthenware pots or rush-baskets, and put together the things that may touch without harm. A pound of meat without paper puts the unprovided purchaser in a dilemma. At the fair there is no dividing line between tradesmen and buying people. Whoever wishes may go and take his place, or he may take no place, and simply hawk his things about through the crowd. There are men hawking old clothes, old boots, iced beer and ices. At ten o'clock in the morning the scene is one of the utmost liveliness. Peasants are standing round the ice-cream men and smacking their lips; would-be purchasers of mutton are standing among the sheep, weighing them and feeling them with their hands in primitive fashion; at the back of the forges meal and flour sellers, white from head to foot, are shovelling their goods into the measures of gossips; girls are raking over the cottons; the cucumber sellers are shouting; and those who have finished their buying are moving off with carts and barrows, sacks or baskets, as the case may be, and not infrequently one may see a man with a sack of potatoes in one hand and a fat sheep under the other arm.

Later in the summer this became a Melon Fair, and later still a Grape Fair. The melons were piled on the ground and resembled heaps of cannon balls, reminding me forcibly of the trophies of 1812 preserved in the Kremlin at Moscow. There were acres of the large melon, that one known as the *arbuse*, dark, swarthy green without, blood crimson within. This is a national fruit. It keeps well, and will be on every peasant's table at Christmas. The deacon at Lisitchansk ate half a melon at every meal when I was there last Christmas. In August they are as plentiful as apples, and sell for a halfpenny or a farthing apiece. There are so many of them that they overflow the towns and the villages; one imagines them rolling away and filling up all the ditches if a wind came in the night. Then their colour is a delight, and it is very pleasant to see the chubby children munching big red chunks of it.

Waggons of grapes, cartloads of honey, in such terms did the season express itself as it grew older. Grapes were two pounds a penny, and honey threepence a pound! And this also was the season of chilis, which were bought in great quantities for pickling. Then vegetable marrows and beetroots overflowed the plain—beetroots too sweet for English palates. Tomatoes were eventually sold by the bucketful. Peaches came and were sold at a penny a pound, and apples at prices that it seems absurd to mention. I said to Alimka one morning, " Let's buy twopennyworth of apples," and we received so many that we had to return home and empty our basket before we could make any more purchases. I should only have bought a farthing's worth. Then a very interesting feature of the fairs were the rosy cherry apples, no bigger than cherries, and very hard, but making a jam that is beautiful and delicious.

It was pleasant to note the preparations for the winter. Stores were being laid in which would not be exhausted even in the spring. The miller was making jam in the yard three times a week; even the Tatar woman below, whom Ali befriends, was taking immense stock of cheap fruit, boiling it for jam or *nalivka*, infusion of fruit, or drying it for *compôte*. Even the *koutia*, which will be eaten on Christmas Eve, was being prepared now. In the yards of all the houses, in the fields about the cottages, cooking and curing and pickling was going forward. Brine was prepared for the cucumbers and the fish, syrup for the jam—Russian housewives always make their jam by preparing a syrup first. Apples cut into squares, wild plums and apricots, were drying on the roofs; chains of onions three yards long, chains of dried mushrooms and baranka biscuits were being hung up on the walls. All day one smelt the savoury odours of food fresh cooked, all day one saw little urchin children like Alimka and Fatima running in and out of doors with tit-bits that they had stolen, or that an indulgent mother had dealt out. The flies buzzed about the doors and windows as if in quest of paradise.

Such is the picture of life in connection with the fairs; the picture is somewhat inadequate, but I hope it may serve to show the feeling there was of abundance. It was an exhilarating element in the atmosphere, and together with the impression of immense mountains and deep wide skies allowed one to live in the large things of life. And Russia is the land of a few large things as opposed to England, a land of many small ones. No disparagement to my native land! Russia is neither greater nor less than England, but it is different.

CHAPTER XXXIV

OVER THE CAUCASUS

1. *Bareback to Kobi*

I HAD given Nicholas an address, Poste Restante, Mleti, and as Mleti is in the province of Tiflis, on the other side of the mountains, it took several days' tramping to get there. I set off one August morning. The following are pages from my diary:

KOBI, 10*th August*, 6 a.m.

I am sitting on the stone wall of a bridge and am spread to the sun. Last night I slept on a ledge of red porphyry rock beside some moss and grasses; the dew was very heavy and I felt cold. I don't think I slept much, but I feel pretty fit at this moment, sitting as I am in the sun on this bridge. I got up at the first sign of dawn and went to one of the inns of the village—each village has several inns of a kind, half grocer's shop and half wine house—*dukhans* they call them. The samovar was actually on the table steaming. Hot tea was wonderful after such a cold night.

This village is six thousand feet up, and I should probably have slept at the posting-station, but I arrived too late last night. So I slept out again as on the last three nights. I had a very lively journey hither. I left the Kazbek Station yesterday evening, and thought to find a comfortable sleeping-place in the barley fields that lay between the road and the River Terek; but just as I was beginning my tramp an Ossetine came up with four horses and asked would I care to ride one. It was a bareback business, and I rather fought shy of it, but he pointed out a quiet horse and assured me we should go gently. We should need to go gently if I was going to feel comfortable after eighteen versts of it. There were of course neither stirrups nor saddle, and as I had a blanket across my back I made a saddle of that. I felt ridiculously stiff in the legs, for I had walked thirty miles already, but I managed to scramble on to the horse's back. The Ossetine disengaged his horse from the other three and rode separately. I had two horses at my side. It was very uncomfortable riding, but I soon learnt what to do; how to kick him if the horse went too slow; how to cry *brrrrr* if I wanted him to stop. But, oh! how sore I got. After five versts I began to ride side-saddle. At six versts we stopped at a wine-shop, another *dukhan;* there are plenty of them along the road. There is no Government monopoly of spirits on this side of the Caucasus. They can't enforce that on a population that has produced its own wines for centuries. I did not much want to stop but the Ossetine

KAZBEK POSTING-STATION

did. He was an unprofitable companion, for utter stupidity he would be hard to be matched; he was almost totally lacking in intelligence. He put on a thoughtful look whenever he was addressed, and answered something irrelevant. I do not think he could understand any sentence in which the word wine did not occur, hence his astonishing imbecility. His face was reminiscent of the sun shining through a shower of rain, eyes and moustache wet-looking, and the latter yellow and shiny—in his eyes fore-knowledge of wine—also remembrance of wine. A boy came out of the *dukhan* and tied our horses to posts. The Ossetine became very gay and festive, and directly he got into the shop slapped the innkeeper on the back, and ordered sixpennyworth of white wine, which meant a bucketful. It had a look of the tea I have made from the Terek when the river has been very muddy, and it was a trifle fiery. I drank two glasses and the man had the rest. When the bucket was dry he began to be very sympathetic with me. I had only had two glasses; what a pity there wasn't any more. Shouldn't we have some red wine now? But I wasn't going to buy him any more wine, and I had a wish to get to Kobi in fairly decent style, so I said, " No thanks, I don't want any more, but if you want another drink you order it; don't be shy on my account. I haven't any more money." This conference had lasted some time; it was getting darker; I did not want to arrive in Kobi after night-fall; it would then be difficult to find a soft place to encamp for the night. But the host brought in tea. This was free of charge, and so we sipped it, and played with it, while the Ossetine tried to persuade me to stand him another bucket of wine. He failed; we went out. He was drunk before we dismounted, and now he was at the fighting stage. He had separated the horses differently at the inn, so that I was with one only; and now, without a word of warning, he slashed them from behind with a whip. We went off at a gallop; he brought his two horses into line, and we went forward neck to neck full pelt for two versts as if we were a desperate cavalry charge. It was fearfully thrilling! We came to a sudden halt at a turn of the road in order to let a cart pass; we were all four horses, all scrunched and cooped up in a corner. The Ossetine swore by all his saints if he had any—he was a Mahommedan—for my horse was backing into him, and kicking out with its hind legs. Then suddenly we left the road and cantered over the moor to the Terek. The river was by no means so impetuous there as in the Dariel Gorge, and we forded it. What a kicking and splashing we made, and how the horses stumbled! I thought I should have been pitched into the water. Of course I got drenched to the knees as it was. After this I had to dismount and put my rug straight, and the first thing that happened after I got on again was most startling—the flame, flash and bang of a revolver just in front of me, and the Ossetine tearing off as if he were possessed. I thought someone had shot at him, especially as he signalled to me over his shoulder. I kicked my steed, brought him along sharply and got abreast of him. It was the Ossetine who had fired, and two minutes later he fired again. The wild man was brandishing his weapon and shouting in his own language. Then he grinned at me, and said in Russian, " No one's going to touch me, eh? " I felt apprehension, and took good care to keep behind him. I did not want a bullet in my back. He continued to flare about, and pull up his horse at unexpected moments, and with such severity that it pawed the air. Presently, whilst we were leading our horses down some steep rocks amid a litter of stones, it seemed he fired at me. I asked him to be careful and he grinned maliciously. Then we re-forded the Terek and regained the road, which was a relief, for there is less chance of being murdered on the highway than among the rocks. The Ossetine became very sulky; he had evidently been long on the way and would be abused by his master when he got to Kobi. No pace was quick enough for him; I think if I had been thrown he would have left me by the wayside and charged ahead full gallop with the four horses. I was glad enough, therefore, when the lights of Kobi appeared. I dismounted outside the village and walked in. The wine and the tea and the gallop made me feel more queer than a rough Channel passage would have done. Then I wished I had some number to write down, that would indicate how tired my legs were of clasping that horse's back.

I slept on the hard rock, or did not sleep, and had hot tea in the morning, and here I am. I shall take things easily to-day.

This is a beautiful place, a wide trough of black earth high up among the mountains. It has an immense sky for a mountain village, and the air is buoyant, fresh, perfect. All around are rosy porphyry rocks, and like a gleam in fairyland the sunlight comes upon them at dawn. This is the village to have a cottage in; it is perfectly beautiful and in the heart of the mountains, and is at cross-roads. Only the flowers are few; perhaps it stands too high. The water flowing under this bridge is green and clear and cold. I have just washed in it. What luxury! Within a stone's throw is a rock out of which gushes seltzer water with iron in solution. According to the natives it cures everything, even the pain that you feel when in the mountains you come across the track of the devil.

2. *Driving a Cart to Gudaour.*

GUDAOUR, 10*th August.*

I have been feeling very saddle-sore, but to-day my pains are too many and too various to describe. I came over the pass on a cart this day, and was so jolted that I felt in need of internal refitting. I had been lying by the roadside at Kobi drinking in the sunshine; it was perfectly blissful. I was determined not to walk to Gudaour; it didn't matter if I did spend a day in perfect idleness. But at noon I was aware of a vehicle crawling towards me up the road, and I thought I would ask a place in it for my weary bones. It took half an hour to come up, however, for the driver was fast asleep and the horse was going at its own sweet will, *i.e.*, at about a mile an hour. I woke the man. He was an Armenian, a copper-coloured fellow with a black eye. When I got in, he beat the horse furiously with a thick cudgel for about half a verst distance, and then relapsed into sleep. We went at a smart pace and then slowed down. The horse kept looking backward all the time—it had no blinkers—watching its master and the angle of his cudgel. When the Armenian was fast asleep the horse resumed its original speed of one mile an hour. And so, laboriously, we climbed the ten versts to Krestovy, the ridge of the pass. The scenery was extremely beautiful and the air very cold and fresh. At Vladikavkaz I expect there were 90 or 100 degrees Fahrenheit, but here, in the shade, it was near freezing-point. The avalanche snow lay in great quantities below us, bridging the little rivers. Even now and then there was snow on the road. But we were protected from snow slides by covered ways at the most important points. The chief feature of the landscape were the cascades. Narrow silvery waterfalls dropped from ledge to ledge of the red porphyry rock. They are the prettiest things I have seen in the Caucasus, for these mountains are the places of the sublime rather than of the charming.

At six versts the Armenian collapsed backward into the cart and then woke up. The horse immediately changed speed to five miles an hour; these collapsings had evidently happened before and been followed by cudgel thumping. The driver now rubbed his eyes, and then looked at me as if seeing me for the first time. Then he seemed to recollect, asked me where I was going to, and gave me the reins. I took the seat in front, for he evidently wanted me to drive. He, for his part, spread his sheepskin cloak in the cart, and snuggled himself to go to sleep. His last words were, " Hit her hard, she's not a horse, she's a devil."

At eight versts I looked behind and saw a strange cloud coming from the north. It looked like a clenched fist, and all the knuckles stood out hard with anger. I took advice and thumped the horse a little. It would not be pleasant to be caught in a storm. We got along at a better pace, the horse squinting back at me to see if I were going to sleep. It was amusing that it increased or slackened its speed as I raised or lowered the stick. It was scarcely necessary to touch the horse at all. I felt I had something in common with the conductor of an orchestra. It was a cunning horse, however, and knew that I was not its master. At the highest point of the road it stopped stock-still and refused to budge;

my mild thumping had no effect. The wind had now risen to a gale and the fist of cloud had become a wide army of vapours. I got down and led the horse a little way, and then hopped to my seat while the cart was in motion. We went like this for half a verst, and then the horse made a sudden dash off the road and settled down to eat grass. More habits were displaying themselves. I got him off after some trouble, and set him going on the road again. This proceeding, which had to be repeated every verst or so, reminded me of the "Innocents Abroad" and the mules. When they wished to change direction they had to dismount, lift up the mules by the hind-quarters, and turn them to the new angles. I expect the mules would then go on a good way without stopping: my case was worse. In six versts we should be at Gudaour and could take shelter, but the rain would overtake us. The clouds were pouring over the rocks and cliffs all about, and only far away to the south spread the blue sky as yet not covered. Suddenly the clouds came drifting over the road; we were obliged to stop, and as they rolled over us and the cart they seemed to turn to rain at a touch. But we were only five minutes in the mist; we heard a long roll of thunder, and suddenly, instead of cloud it was hissing, stinging hail. The Armenian slept soundly, and I wrapped myself in my blanket and urged the horse forward. The road lay downhill and we moved quickly towards Gudaour. In an hour we arrived there and the rain had stopped; the clouds had passed over our heads and there was blue sky again. The sun shone.

We stopped at an inn in the village, and, looking down from there, could see the thunderstorm that had left us raging in the valleys of Mleti and Ananour. The clouds were literally below us, and we saw the blue sky above them. How brightly the sun shone! it stood just beyond a little grassy summit where some sheep were browsing; it seemed that if one were there one could stretch out one's hand and take it from its place.

The Armenian had definitely wakened up now and was preparing to have a good meal. The innkeeper lit a wood fire on the stone floor of his dwelling and prepared to do some cooking. We bargained for a chicken between us. It would cost sixpence. The chicken was already plucked, and the innkeeper threw it into a pot that he had on the fire. Whilst we waited for it to cook we had a bucket of red wine before us, and the Armenian did himself justice.

"You're an Englishman," said he. "You ought to know where there's any war going on. Where's there any war, I say? Where's there any war?"

"In Spain," I suggested. "The Spanish are fighting the Moors."

"I never heard of it; there's been a war here, you know, in Persia, but Persians are weak fellows, and the Russians are weak. Three Persians one Russian, three Russians one Armenian. Loris Melikoff, eh? Did you ever hear of him? He was the greatest general the Russians ever had, and he was an Armenian. The richest man in the world is an Armenian. He lives in London and keeps a flying machine. You are English, why don't you use a flying machine? What does the sky look like in England? Is it full of machines? One day I shall go there. Already I know some English, *brodt, bootter*. The English are better than the Russians. Fine machines they have. But they break down, oh, they break down. I saw two yesterday that couldn't get on. How would you like to plough a mountain side with one of your machines? You'd break down. But a horse wouldn't break down; a horse for me. Do you know they wanted me to join the army, serve my time, be drilled, learn to ride and shoot. I said to the General, ' The devil comes to me to learn to ride and shoot, who's going to give me lessons? No Russian. I should think not. Why,' I said, ' you give me your hat and I'll put it on one of these mountain peaks so far away that you can't see it, far less fire at it, but I'll take a gun and shoot it off.' He said, ' We shall have to have you all the same,' but they wont. I'll go to England or America first. Don't I wish there'd come a war; we Armenians would throw off the Russians and have our own king. Dirty, vodka-drinking Russians, always begging or drinking. Directly a Russian finds five copecks he runs as hard as he can to the public-house and drinks vodka, and when he comes out of the shop, if he sees a rich man coming, he will stand at the side of the road and say 'Give me five copecks.' Shameless people!"

The arrival of the chicken cut short this harangue, of which I have only remembered a little. He turned out to be a wonderful conversationalist, this little man, who seemed to be without words altogether when we were in the cart. The chicken was tender. It was served to us without knives and forks and on one plate; we each took bones and picked them like heathens; with the chicken there were pickled gherkins and white bread and home-made cheese. The samovar appeared and we had tea.

3.

MLETI.

I slept under a rock last night. A large boulder had fallen on three other rocks and made a little cavern. One had to let oneself in very gingerly, for the opening was so small. It felt like sliding into a letter-box to sleep. But the bottom was soft sand and the place was secure from men and from rain. I was soaked through; my blanket weighed at least a hundredweight with the water that was in it. But I slept. This morning I have been drying myself. My blanket is open wide to the sun and is steaming. I have taken my coat off, and it also is lying on a rock getting dried.

By road to Mleti it is eighteen versts; cross-country

MLETI

it is only five. I came across country accordingly. But it is a very difficult matter, Mleti being 2500 feet lower. The road zig-zags extraordinarily, and I crossed it six times before getting to this valley.

Mleti is verdant. It is pleasant to get into a land of leaves and flowers after two days among the desolate, barren passes. And there is no river. Consequently there is extraordinarily stillness and peace. It is the first time I have been out of hearing of a river since I have been in the Caucasus. I am sitting on a bank where sweet-scented violets are growing; the air is filled with their perfume. There are hollyhocks on the slopes, hundreds and thousands of them, some over six feet high, and covered with saffron-coloured blossoms. I came through some weeds so high that they closed above my head and shut out the sky, a waste of dead nettle, comfrey, teasel, canterbury bells and convolvulus. Clusters of pink mallow hung like bouquet-baskets from these tangles. On the rocks there is an abundance of stone-crop and bryony and pinks which look like sweet-williams. The rock-roses are perfect gems. High up, near Gudaour, I found several plants which could not have been other than tradescantia, which is not supposed to grow wild out of Asia. But there is no end to the wild flowers of the Caucasus, and plants brought up with tender care in England grow brightly and abundantly without any care at all on these wildernesses.

There were three letters from Nicholas; he has saved up money and thinks of going to London again. They are highly characteristic letters, full of poetry. The first one begins, " And someone has moved a stone with his accursed hand," which sounds very tragical in the Russian of Lermontof. It means, I think, that Fate has separated two friends who ought never to have been put asunder. Later on in his letter he writes, " For you the road to happiness lies open, for me it is closed for ever." This sentence reminded me of the day when he plastered up the mirror with newspaper so that he shouldn't see his face. He proposes that I come to Lisitchansk in the autumn, and that we return from there to London. " Couldn't I go, if only for a month? "

EPILOGUE

ON my way back I found a cottage at Kobi for next summer. It is made of stone and has two rooms. A sparkling rivulet comes past, washing, as it were, the toes of the cottage. It will be empty if I come and claim it in the spring, and I think I shall. Now my summer draws to a close. Already the procession of autumn has commenced: the trees at the summits of the mountains have turned from green to golden. The messenger has come to Proserpine. Presently, where I used to count five snowy peaks, I shall find seven and then ten, till at last the little Sphinx mountain that squats outside Vladikavkaz will also be a peak and glisten like the rest. The thorn-apples have already burst and thrown out their crimson seed, and like dusty yellow balls the Cape gooseberries have appeared on the mountains. The glories of gold and brown have spread downwards like fire into the valleys. The leaves are falling from the trees on the hills where the wind roars, from the trees in the valleys, even from the trees in the town, where there is no wind at all, and the snow is descending in the valleys. The sleet falls in Vladikavkaz, and then snow, and then in November even Vladikavkaz is, as Moscow and St Petersburg and the whole wintry north, a snow-clad town. The cycle of seasons has gone round; winter turned to slush on Palm Sunday at Moscow, it changed to laughing spring on the hill-slopes at Vladikavkaz. Summer followed the plough over the fields and blushed in a myriad flowers. The maize fields waved, the sunflowers gazed. Then autumn was seen in the streets, whilst all the village folk threshed the corn with flails. The priest blessed the first fruits and autumn was past. Once more it became the turn of winter, the most Russian of all seasons. Quick pace the winter came just as it had passed away. As in the spring sledges gave way to wheels in a day, so now did the wheels give way and the sledge ruled the road.

A wave of intense longing came and I must see England again. So one day found me once more in the city of fog and rain. As I walked down Fleet Street in Russian attire I heard someone say, "There goes a Pole." But when I came into the city people were not deceived, and despite my shabby soft black hat, unclipped hair, and furry overcoat, a young man in Throgmorton Street persisted in whistling behind me that Gilbert and Sullivan air:—

"Oh, he might have been a Rooshian,
A Greek, a Turk, a Prooshian,

> But in spite of all temptati-on
> To belong to another nati-on
> *He was an Englishman!"*

Yes, he was.

The time comes to draw a line and strike a balance, and that is not an easy thing to do. Life to me has meant love, and, as Antony says, "there's beggary in love that can be measured." My gains are not to be set down. Many things are true until they are set down in words. A pressed flower is not a flower at all.

I went to Russia to see the world, to see new life, to breathe in new life. In truth it was like escaping from a prison, and now when I take a walk in London streets it seems as if I am taking the regulation exercise in a prison yard. And the dirty rags of London sky look like a tramp's washing spread on the roofs to dry. Still, it is given that we live even in prisons and under such skies for certain purposes. The towns have their beauties and mysteries even as the mountains have. I, least of all, have reason to be despondent there, for, like the companion of Christian, I have in my bosom that key which is called Promise.

At my room in the mill at Vladikavkaz I commonly looked out upon three pictures. In the foreground was a row of trembling poplars, and beyond these was a beautiful soft green hill, and beyond all a great grey mystic range of mountains. I call them the Present, the Future and the Eternal. The pleasant waving poplars were very real, very clear, and every leaf stood out distinctly, but on the green hill the trees were so many that I could not pick one out and see it clearly. It tempted me to go there and explore. The hill was full of allurement and charm, as it were, of the deep eyes of a woman as yet unknown but destined to be loved. It betrayed a mystery which it did not reveal.

Moreover, the green hill seemed to be the best standing place for looking into that vision of the eternal, of the ever-present mystery of Man and his Life. The mountains seemed to be the Ikon in God's open-air room, His vast chamber of Nature.

Here then is the story of my life and of its gains written in the terms of these symbols. It was written at the Mill, it is a flower wreath gathered on the mountains.

The Horizon

A youth steps forward on the road and a horizon goes forward. Sometimes slowly the horizon moves, sometimes in leaps and bounds. Slowly while mountains are approached, or when cities and markets crowd the skies to heaven, but suddenly and instantaneously when summits are achieved or when the outskirts dust of town or fair is passed. One day, at a highest point on that road of his, a view will be disclosed and lie before him—the furthest and most magical glance into the

Future. Away, away in the far-distant grey will lie his newest and last horizon, in a place more fantastic and mystical than the dissolving city, which the eye builds out of sunset clouds.

Time was when the youth played carelessly in a meadow and knew not of the upward road and mountainous track. The destiny which was his had spoken not from bee or flower; and if it came to him, came only as a dream-whisper in the soft breeze that now and then fluttered in his ears. The sun was then his, the blue sky and the field below, and flower and leaf and tree and the glad air. As these belonged to him, so he also belonged to them, and neither knew nor cared of the having or the losing. Life was joy, and joy was life. But mornings pass, and every noon is a turning-point. One afternoon found him wending from the meadow and bending steps towards a green slope that lay before him, cool and fresh and tempting. By a foot-path over the hill he went to the great high road. The grasses waved farewell to him as the evening breeze ruffled them in the sunlight. The green slope parted with him, and he left its sunlight and freshness, and his eyes looked on the road. What was there in the road that he should leave the hill for her—that he should take its dust for her? He knew not, neither questioned he, but moved ahead towards the highway which stretched out over the undulating plain far up into the west; towards the highway which led to the land of the setting sun, and which lost itself in a region of crimson and gold. For the sun went down to the level of the plain, and for a moment appeared as the very gateway through which at last the great road gave into enchanted regions. Onward the youth sped gaily, light in his face, life in his steps, the songs of the meadow-birds in his heart. Some spell in the road drew him onward, or some meaning wrought in him impelled him forward. Onward he sped on the long upward road, and gained its first incline as the sunset faded away. Then had the horizon faded inward near him, and all became grey and lonely as he gained the next incline, and then a summit gained, the first summit giving view to further slope and further crest. He now left the land of plains and upward made his path, and only seldom descended into valleys; but as night came on, and with night wistfulness and loneliness, he looked about him where he should find rest. He lay down in the grass by the roadside, and the fresh odour in the grass brought back the meadow thoughts, and a certain staleness and dustiness came as sadness upon his heart. And as he lay watching the starlight growing brighter in the grey sky, he dreamed uneasily of the gay meadow and its flies and bees, and of the red sunset-gate, and of something appalling, though mysterious, there.

Many days followed this day, and the youth had lain on many banks of the same long dusty road, when one afternoon a change came over him. He had tired early, for the noonday sun had been terrible, and the hot road hard to his way-weary feet. He had lain among the long fresh grasses beside a bush of the wild rose, and had fallen asleep. Weary had he been, and the world had seemed dull to him, the road ever the same, the sky the same, village and town the same, and nowhere was there beauty and freshness and new delight. Not seven days a week were there for him but to-day, name it what one would, eternally recurred. He fell asleep among the grasses. But when he woke it was in a surprise, for the world had changed. Away in the west the sun had set mildly and a little moon had risen; a tender night breeze was on the wing, and earliest moths flitted from bush to tree. He awakened, or rather he and himself awakened, a self below himself had awakened, as if the soul had drawn curtains from two windows after a long custom of drawing from only one. A new being waking, blinked uneasily to find itself in the swing and motion of life. "Who set me going?" it asked, for it had power to ask questions that the first being could not answer. The road stretched out an eternity before and an eternity behind, but he knew not why, and could give no answer to the questions: What is the road? Whither leads the road? Whence comes the road? Where did you begin to march upon it? Why did you leave the meadow? To all these questions answer such as could be given was forthcoming, and was unsatisfactory enough withal. Long into night brooded the two beings together, and then for weariness forgot and slept. And the next morn both awoke and took this road, upon which his steps had become a habit. Now all was thought and question, and the youth found a new use for the wayfarers he met, and not a tradesman or pilgrim or petty trafficker upon the road but he put to him his questions concerning the destiny which was at the end of the way. To most these questions were too difficult. Not a few said there was no answer, not a few said there was no question. Many would have persuaded him that he sought a mere shadow, a phantom, an illusion. Many bade him give up the quest and settle upon the roadside in some town or village. "Then I should be lost!" said the youth. "For I have left a home which I can never find again, in order that I may find a home which my heart tells me shall be mine, and there is no rest for me till my mind agrees with my heart." Then on one occasion an old pilgrim answered, "Knowest thou not, my son, that this road leads eternally round the world? So long is it, and so hard, that by old age thou canst only win back to the sight of the land where thou wast once a child. Be advised, quit the road where thou must always be a seeker. Abandon thy quest, and settle here where the pleasant stream gently flows under the red stone bridge of the village. Thou wilt be lost, but thou wilt sleep and forget, and one morning will find thee once more the happiness lost in leaving the meadow."

Yet the youth pressed on, and the seasons passed by, and the years rolled over with whites and greens and reds and browns. Years passed, and still upon the road the young man moved, and at length fewer people appeared—fewer communities—less used and worn the road appeared. One night he came to a hermit's hut. His old question he put to the hermit, but the latter was a mocker. " Why is this road here; did not God make it? Oh, my very young man, this road wasn't made by God—man made it; this is *the beaten track,* the way man has followed man and sheep has followed sheep through all time. This is the safest road round the road and back again. The wheel of sunlight rolls evenly along it, down over it in the west in the evening, and up again in the east in the morning. To the sun every inch of its road is known, and there are no discoveries to be made upon it, no new things to be found. Thou mightst have in the meadow learnt all its secrets from the sun. But men find happiness along the road, some in the hope of finding the new, others in foot-measuring its miles, and some become happy resting by the road, and settling there, and again others have their joy in the nourishment of a secret hope of finding the goal of the road. The sun provides the best happiness, and does all the work that needs to be done, and from mankind he has no need of help to rule the world. Be not over anxious, my son, about goals and aims and objects; they are only the vessels of happiness. And I counsel you, bethink you, now that the road becomes more solitary, that your hope may become a burden or may become too small. I also was of your spirit, and persevered far along the road till I lost my hope and had no means of happiness. In the hermit's hut one learns the art of being happy. One fashions the soul to the deepest of all cups. . . ."

But the youth interrupted: "You have been along the road, father! Tell me of that, for it is my road, and nought can discourage me from my wish to know its end and meaning." The hermit smiled. "Soon you come to a land of towers," he said. "The towers were set up by happy seekers; much time they spent in building, and much secret happiness they gained thereby. Watch-towers they are, and places of survey, besides many league-stones and markers of progress. But really, now, there are no more towers to be built, I think. Far as I went along the road I found towers, and, indeed, nought but towers at last. And ever as thou comest to a new tower, thou, like myself long since, wilt climb the stairs and take survey, and see a next tower—watch-towers both—and from either only barren road and watch-tower visible. These are not the profitable reaches of the road of wisdom."

The morning after this the wanderer rose after calm sleep. New hope was in his eyes, and a new thought in his heart. "This is *the beaten track*," he said, as he stamped in the dust, and he was gay, though he knew not the reason of his gaiety. Light of heart was he, and happiness danced in his steps. But about noon clouds came over the sky, and his gaiety gave way to a new questioning and a new seriousness. He began to see that he was coming to a more desolate country. Naught was there before the eye but sky and road, and then at length a first tower. Then he mounted to the highest look-out and searched the land to the new horizon, but the view was blank; only as a speck far onward on the road he dimly made out the form of a second tower. "I am weary of the road," he said, as he turned to descend the stairs, and when he had got to the foot a confession was on his lips that the hermit was right. Progress along the road was but vanity and vexation of spirit. Now from sunset to dawn was a desolate land of road and dust and towers all the way from west to east. A strange weariness and anger possessed his soul, and it happened that he saw a bank, and feeling that all wish to go on had vanished he threw himself down upon it. So he lay beside the road and fought with despair and weariness. Far over the wide country his eye wandered, but found no resting-place. As the sun set stormily and angrily he looked away to the north and scanned the sombre plain, and then restlessly turned to the south. His heart brooded over some wrong, and his mind sought some object to provoke it to thought. His eye wandered over the desert to the south, and settled on a soft purple line that lay at the horizon. No window of the tower faced south, or he might have been tempted to mount its steps once more; for of a sudden the wrong was gone from his heart, the seeking from his mind, and the restlessness from his spirit. In place of these had come a new energy, a new longing, a new love. Still he sat hesitating by the bank, and suddenly new thoughts flooded his mind as joy suffused his heart. "This *was* my road; this *is* my road no longer. My heart brought me so far, but I am no further tempted along its dust; now towards the desert my heart yearneth. This is the beaten track, and beyond this point I, too, would be merely following, heartlessly helpless, like a loose stone down the steep slope of time." For awhile he dwelt in the peace of his own heart. Then a sunbeam flashed from beyond a cloud, and like a searchlight lit up the way about him, and he saw what he had not discerned before, that the road, though apparently one and continuous away to the west, branched by an ill-defined track away to the south also. Then the old magic came back, and he knew that for him the true road was this one diverging to the south, this unworn way, this little-traversed path to the purple mountains.

. . . .

A youth steps forward on a new road and a horizon goes forward. Sometimes slowly the horizon moves, sometimes in leaps and bounds; slowly while mountain is neared, suddenly when crests are achieved. The enchantment which of old drew him from the meadow to the hill, and from hill to highway, still goes before him, enticing him forward. Life loves him and flees before him, and as with the eyes of a woman looks out and beckons him. She is the secret mistress of his heart; as yet she is unknown, her love unrevealed, her mystery and meaning unexplored.

Over brown moors and mountains green the wanderer clambers, and sighs his soul to the goal that for the present stands before all others in the sky. Over the ridges he passes and surmounts the rocks and passes with light steps along the higher slopes, and then arduously battles among crag and boulder, abyss and great rock. . . .

And the conqueror is at last ascending the final darkest, highest crag of all; only blackness is before him, and adamantine rock. All horizon is gone; there is no future but the future in his heart. Then suddenly the worst becomes the best; the darkest the brightest; the narrowest the widest; the shortest the furthest. The conqueror stands with his foot upon the mountain's brow, and all the kingdoms of the world lie beneath him. He has risen as a sun upon his own world, the dawn whereby he sees his life has come. Now dwells he in the eternal blue of ether, and looks down with pity to the clouds below and the mists of fields and fogs of cities, to the places where those live who did not believe in their quests or in his. Now he learns the utmost limit of the meaning of human life, and he can renounce beyond knowledge in his sufficiency. In nothing more shall he ever be surprised. Life is revealed, the woman who fled is won. Now is the horizon removed to its utmost possibility—further than that grey-blue line he cannot pass. He may descend the mountain, but the horizon will narrow on—narrow in, and even though it widen out again, and although he run his life's journey along the way, he will win no further than these, for that is the shore of life itself, on which rolls the grey sea of Death.

As he descends into the plains, happiness remains his, and the mountain vision remains in his heart. Life has been revealed; now it shall be explored. Now he shall learn in detail the mystery in each contribution of each little plot to that grand mountain harmony that flashed before his vision as he reaches his topmost peak. He shall learn in detail the meaning of those distant greys and blues. He may take what path he chooses—north or east, or south or west; one path is his and he will choose it. He may meet his old acquaintances of the road, but will have no problems for them to solve. He may see the old villages and cities, but without impatience will he dwell in them, for he has the satisfaction required.

The youth stands and gazes, and all sinks into him. Softly his eyes rest on the herds grazing in the valley, on the great highway, on church and village, on many a green and brown and golden acre lying open to the full kiss of the sky, and many a misty moor and jagged sultry headland—looks over a long grey ridge marked with steeples here and there, and beyond these, to new blues and greys and purples. He measures life; the present to the ultimate future, "the cloud-capped towers, the gorgeous palaces, the solemn temples, the great globe itself," all these to the insubstantial pageant fading in the sleep of dreams.

APPENDIX

HOW TO GET ABOUT

A Chapter for Prospective Tourists

THERE seems to me to be every reason why Englishmen should visit the Caucasus and see what it is like for themselves. There is no likelihood of the place being overrun, or of ordinary pleasure-seekers invading it. The Caucasus is a preserved Alps.

I propose to write a few words on the facilities for seeing the country in the hope that they may be of use to some who think of touring there.

The fare from London to Vladikavkaz is:

1st class return . .	£19
2nd ,, ...	£13
3rd ,, . . .	£8, 10s.

Return tickets are available for sixty days.

The tickets cannot be taken right through, and it is advisable to take them from London to Alexandrovo, the Russian frontier, and thence to Vladikavkaz. There are various companies which issue tickets for

Alexandrovo, the Great Eastern Railway Company, the London, Chatham and Dover, and the Belgium States Railway Company, 52 Gracechurch Street, E.C. The last-named is the only company issuing third-class tickets. It is as convenient to travel third as to travel second in Belgium and Germany. In Russia, however, it is extremely inconvenient to travel third class. The carriages are dirty, and the passengers Russian peasants, and the seats are wooden. First and second-class compartments are very comfortable, and one may be fairly sure of sleeping at night, since a ticket entitles one to the whole length of a seat.

The train takes five days from Alexandrovo, with changes at Warsaw (here one has to cross the town from the Viensky to the Brestky Station, the fare for which by droshky is one rouble), Kiev, Poltava and Rostof. There is, however, a fast train, Warsaw-Rostof (first and second class only), which enables one to do the journey in two days less. A special ticket (platzkaart), costing 10s., has to be bought at the Brestky Station, Warsaw. The train leaves that station at 5.11 p.m.

Another route is by train to Odessa (tickets may be taken from London to Odessa), and thence by boat to Novorossisk, Sukhum or Batum.

The fares are:

Port.	Novorossisk.			
Class.	With Meals.		Without Meals.	
	1st	2nd	2nd	3rd
Fare from Odessa in Russian or English Money	27.30 roubles or £2, 17/-	19.90 roubles or £2, 12/-	14.40 roubles or £1, 10/-	5.45 roubles or 12/-
	Sukhum.			
Fare from Odessa in Russian or English Money	38.15 roubles or £3, 19/-	27.50 roubles or £2, 18/-	19.40 roubles or £2, 11/-	6.50 roubles or 14/-
	Batum.			
Fare from Odessa in Russian or English Money	42.10 roubles or £4, 7/-	30.30 roubles or £3, 3/-	21.19 roubles or £2, 15/-	7.50 roubles or 15/-

Another route is *via* St Petersburg and Moscow. Boats carry passengers to St Petersburg at various fares, and the ticket to Vladikavkaz from St Petersburg costs:

(Single)	1st class . .	46 roubles 20 copecks or £4, 15s.
	2nd class . .	26 roubles 95 copecks or £2, 16s.
	3rd class . .	15 roubles 40 copecks or £1, 11s.

It is a long and tiring journey, and one will appreciate the pleasure of lounging in Vladikavkaz for a few days. The hotels are good, and rooms can be taken from a rouble (two shillings) a day. From Vladikavkaz the celebrated Georgian road runs to Tiflis—150 miles. There are various conveyances, and I append the fares:

By motor omnibus from the Grand Hotel .	30 roubles .	1 day
By diligence coach	10 ,, .	2 days
By carriage and pair	70 ,, .	2 ,,
By four-seated lineika (jaunting-car) .	45 ,, .	3 ,,
By furgon (a van)	3 ,, .	4 ,,

(This last must be bargained for beforehand.)

Night accommodation at the post-stations is free, except for a charge of 3d. or 4d. for linen.

Instead of going by any of these conveyances one may walk, and in that way the tourist will undoubtedly see more of the country and of the people. Any passing cart will give one a lift at the rate of about 12 miles for 6d. Food of a rough kind is obtainable at the *dukhans*, of which there are hundreds; bread is 1¼d. (5 copecks) a pound, and eggs (cooked) two a penny or less; wine, 1d. a glass; milk as in England; tea, *ad lib*, 2½d.; mutton, 2½d. a plate; chicken, 3d. or 4d. a plate. [A Russian copeck corresponds to an English farthing, and a rouble is 100 copecks and is approximately worth 2s.] For a rouble one can get an ordinary hot Russian dinner at the post stations. Tiflis hotels are on a level with those of Vladikavkaz—the best is the *Vetsel*, with rooms from one to eight roubles a day.

The Trans-Caucasian railway runs from Tiflis to Batum, a distance of three hundred miles, and passes through some of the most beautiful of the southern country. It runs via Kutais, and this town is connected with Vladikavkaz by a road two hundred miles long, which one may travel partly by stage coach from Kutais to Oni—110 versts, fare about six roubles. The road onward is only open to traffic from June to September, and there are no regular conveyances. One can take a lineika for thirty roubles. The lineika is a low jaunting car, having no protection either against wind or rain. One sits sideways, and one's feet dangle beside the wheels. It has springs and is comfortable enough in fine weather. It is the best vehicle available on this road. The journey over the Mamison Pass, 9281 feet high, may be extremely cold and stormy, and it is advisable to start in the finest weather. A snowstorm in midsummer is by no means unusual. Near Lisri there is a by-road of extraordinary grandeur to Kobi on the Georgian road.

To see *Elbruz* it is best to go to Kislovodsk by rail from Vladikavkaz (260 versts). Kislovodsk is the most fashionable watering-place in Russia.

It is extremely interesting to go by boat from Novorossisk to Batum, calling at each of the thirteen Caucasian ports on the Black Sea—Gilendzhik, Dzhubra, Tuapse, Lazarevsky, Sochi, Adler, Gagri, Gudaut, Novy Afon, Sukhum, Ochemchiri, Batum.

From Sukhum there is a road to Kislovodsk, 300 versts, crossing the Klukhorsky Pass, 9600 feet high.

One can generally obtain a conveyance at the rate of three roubles a day, and the journey, if continuous, would take about ten days. It is possible, however, to do it in four days in a phaeton, and this would cost not less than 100 roubles for the journey. In many places this so-called road degenerates to a mere track broken by rocks and overwashed by waterfalls. It is certainly more convenient to drive than to walk in the higher parts.

Besides these roads there are hundreds of tracks leading to the fastnesses of the mountains, and these are more or less difficult and wild. They can only be explored by the horseman or the pedestrian, and the former needs to have a sure seat. Horses may be hired at £2 for the summer, or may be bought entirely at prices ranging from £5 upwards. It may be mentioned, however, that the natives, especially the Ingooshi, are expert horse thieves.

Russian is the only language of any value in the Caucasus, and the tourist should know at least a smattering of it. It is most important to realise that the natives speak an extremely childish and simple language that is easily understood. It is unnecessary to know more than the elements of the language and a good assortment of useful words. A Berlitz course, or something similar, taught by a Russian teacher, is probably the most useful. One should certainly carry a pocket dictionary.

Much is said of the danger of travelling in the Caucasus, especially by Russians, but there is truly little danger. It is likely that an English traveller will have queer adventures, but unlikely that he will come to harm. I never took my revolver out once on my tramps, but doubtless many people would feel more secure with a weapon in their pocket. One thing may be warned—keep out of the way of the police. The whole police system of the Caucasus is corrupt, and innocent or guilty, English or Russian, one is not likely to get out of their hands easily. Permission to carry firearms into Russia must be obtained through the Russian Consul General in London, and application should be made six weeks in advance.

The outfit may be best purchased in England, but the black sheepskin cloaks worn by many people in the Caucasus are extremely serviceable, being warm and completely waterproof; they can be bought in the towns for ten roubles. It is well to look passably well-dressed on the road, as that ensures respect and courteous treatment. Good manners help one immensely in any difficulty. There is a sort of custom in Russia when entering a shop to salute the shopkeeper and say "Zdrast-vit-yé!" I, for my part, when tramping, would always bow comprehensively to the shopkeeper and the company in the shop—especially if it is an inn.

On entering a shop, a Russian commonly inquires the price of everything there, and the shopman doesn't feel vexed if, after turning over all his wares, nothing is bought. Whereas, if one merely buys a penny glass of wine and drinks it politely, one is wished well on one's journey, the whole company is pleased, and when one goes away the innkeeper says, " There goes an Englishman—a fine man! "

THE END

INDEX